WRITE ME A SIGN

WRITE ME A SIGN
about language experience   LORRAINE WILSON

NELSON

First published in Australia in 1979
Reprinted January 1980, August 1980, 1982, 1983, 1986, 1988, 1990

Thomas Nelson Australia
102 Dodds Street
South Melbourne 3205

© Lorraine Wilson 1979

Photographs by Keith Pigdon

National Library of Australia
Cataloguing in Publication data:
  Wilson, Lorraine
  Write me a sign.
  Index
  ISBN 0 17 005669 4

  1. English language – study and teaching
  (Elementary) I. Title.
  372.6'044

Typeset by ProComp Productions Pty Ltd, Adelaide
Printed in Hong Kong

Contents

Preface vii

1 About children being interested in writing and reading 1

2 About the language experience approach 11

3 About oral language 27

4 About the experiences a teacher may draw upon to develop children's language 37

5 About classroom practice for teaching writing and reading from personal experience 47

6 About the use of published materials 61

7 About the place of phonics 67

8 A suggested literacy course outline 77

Appendix I A case study: Language for thinking 89

Appendix II Checklist of dos and don'ts 97

References 99

Index 101

Preface

I have written this book for teachers and unashamedly describe practice. My specific concern is developing literacy from first-hand experiences or, as it is commonly called, the language experience approach. Of course a language experience approach is an approach for developing listening and speaking as well as reading and writing. I do devote one chapter to developing oral language in the classroom and I have been in a dilemma as to where to place it in the book. That chapter is near the front of the book but readers may choose to read it in some other order.

I spent five years at Northcote Primary School (Helen Street) as Vice Principal, and I have drawn mainly upon my work there. Northcote School is 105 years old and is in inner-suburban Melbourne. The buildings are old and dilapidated. The yard is hopelessly small and ugly. Six hundred pupils attend the school and of these over seventy per cent are from migrant families. Each year just over half the children beginning school speak no English at all. Most of the small percentage of Australian pupils come from working-class families. Over recent years dedicated teachers have implemented an experience-based programme at the school. What an exciting place it is now and how the children love their school!

Because my recent practice has been in an inner-suburban school with working-class pupils, the examples used reflect a particular kind of language. I state most emphatically, however, that the language experience approach is not only suited to poorer, less-able pupils. It is an approach suited to all pupils. All children love to read and write about themselves, so the general approach could be the same for all, while the specifics would vary greatly: the experiences would differ, language usage would differ, teacher expectations would differ. Because the approach is centred in the child and develops from him, only his capabilities set the limits; not arbitrary age norms nor the contents of commercial programmes. I repeat that the language experience approach is a programme for children of varying environments, varying cultures and varying competencies. To avoid confusion throughout the text I refer to the teacher as 'she' and the pupil as 'he' unless speaking about a particular teacher or child.

Melbourne 1979　　　　　　　　　　　　Lorraine Wilson

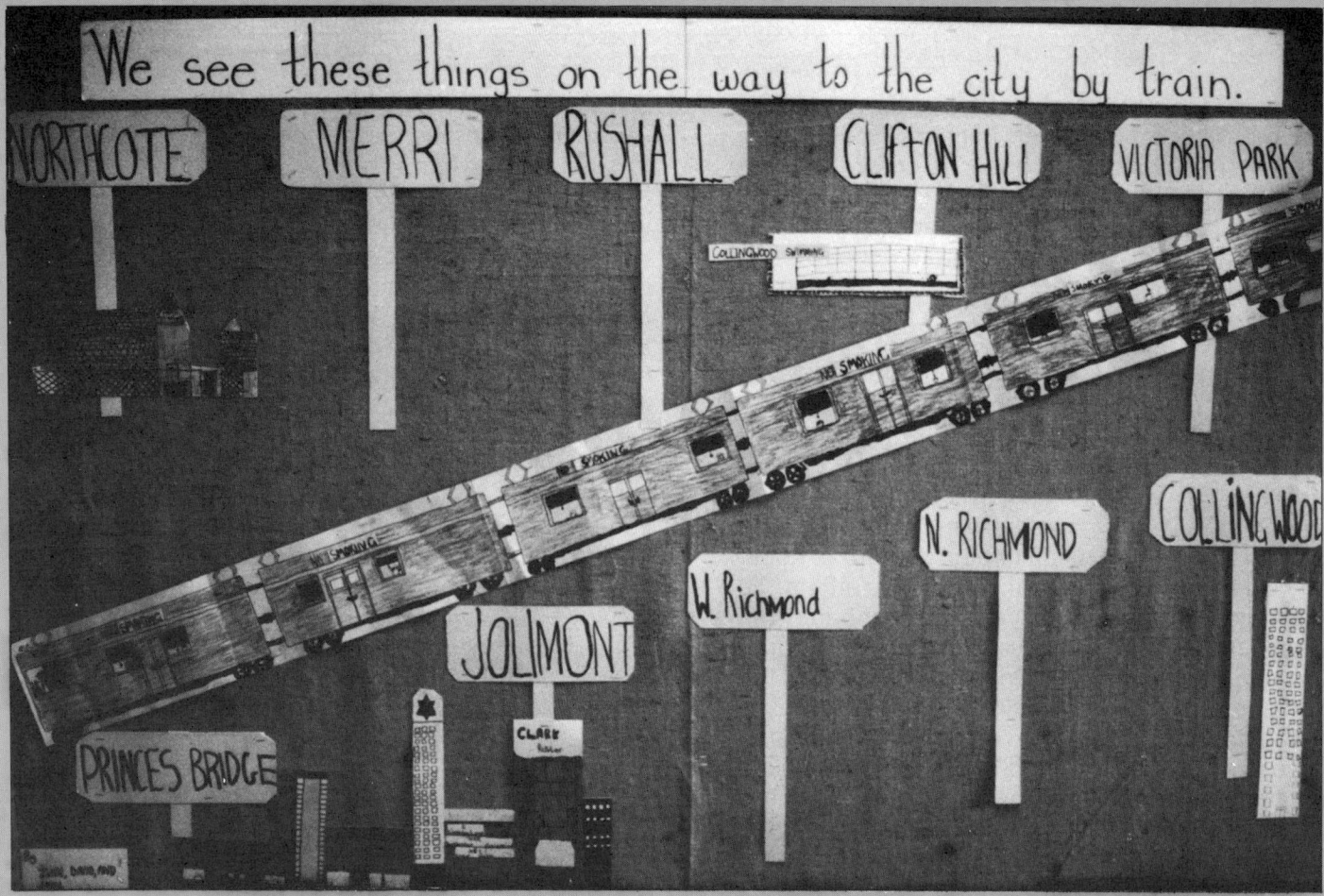

About children being interested in writing and reading

'Write me a sign', says a little voice as I walk across the hall. Again, 'Please write me a sign', and a little hand pulls at my arm. Alex is five and in his first year at school. He has been working hard in the building area during the morning with pleasing results to him. He now has a cubby-house into which he can crawl and hide. He knows that if a sign is pinned to it there is some chance of the cubby staying put for the rest of the day and so, at his direction, I write

Please leave this building.

Alex.

Alex is a little boy who knows what writing is and sees purpose in it.

Shane, Leigh and Jamie are in their third year at school. They too have come to know that there is value in being able to write. They wrote their own sign and attached it to their building.

Shanne and Leigh and
Ples DO NOt tach
Jamie
arn Bildin
Room 18

Craig, in his second year at school, also knows that there is purpose in print. Craig is not yet attempting to write for himself but after completing a cubby he dictated his message to Glenn, a classmate, who wrote for him as follows

There is only fore pepel alawd to play in the cuby hoes no mor then fore pepel. Do not brak it up if eny pepel brokit Crag madeit and the Miss Rakih will growl ath pepel to.

Notice that Glenn has used drawings of four people to indicate to those children who cannot read just how many children can play in the cubby.

Santino started school unable to speak any English at all. In his third year at school he and a friend were in trouble for taking and eating a smaller child's bag of chips. Each of the offenders was asked to bring half the cost of the packet of chips to school the next day. In my office during the day I found this note!

Santino also knew that there was value in being able to write and read and he put his developing skill in writing to good use.

Motivation to Read and Write

Writing and reading must be seen to have value for the learner and, before the learner can see the value in being able to read and write, he first has to know what reading and writing are. It cannot be assumed

Miss wilson
ThS is The muhi for The chips Sanrino
¢5

that children entering school know these things. If children have never seen their parents or someone very close to them read or write, they will have very little knowledge about reading and writing. Why would such five-year olds want to learn to read and write on school entry? The child who does not know what reading is, certainly won't know what a word is. The type of activity in which the teacher flashes single words or letters on flash cards will be quite meaningless to him. Any group of children beginning school may contain children who have never been read to and who have no concepts at all about print, along with five-year-olds who are actually reading.

Individual Differences

How inappropriate it is for a beginners' teacher to have certain class standards or expectations which all those five-year-olds are to meet. The teacher who says at the commencement of the school year, 'I don't believe in pushing beginners. None of these beginners will be introduced to reading until Grade 1', is making the same mistake as the teacher who says, 'All of these beginners will read by the end of the year'. Each of these teachers is applying one standard of performance to all the children in her class. Instead she should observe each child in her class and find answers to the following questions.

Which children do not speak English?
Which children understand only a little English?
Which children are not able to speak in sentences?
Are there any children who are too shy to speak at all?
Which children do not know what books are, what print is, what reading is?
Which children can write their own names?
Which children know what reading and writing are and are eager to learn to do both?
Which children can read already?
Which children have parents who are over-anxious about their children learning to read and write?

It is not difficult to find answers to these questions. When the teacher engages in talk with the children she will soon learn which children do not speak English, which children can speak fluently and confidently, which speak in single word utterances, or which will not speak at all. When reading a storybook she can soon discover which concepts about print the children have if she asks them to point to the cover, the page, the print, the picture, a word and to point with a finger along the page in the direction she should write. As well she should observe those children who can write their own names and who spend a lot of time in the book corner looking at books. Once the teacher has answers to the questions above she can plan goals appropriate to the needs and abilities of each pupil.

HOW TO MOTIVATE CHILDREN FOR INTEREST IN WRITING AND READING

- Aim to have each child develop a positive self image.
- Read good quality story books aloud frequently.
- Read aloud nursery rhymes, nonsense rhymes and movement rhymes for the children to move to.
- Have attractive picture books in the classroom for the children to handle. Change this collection of

books regularly. Bulk borrow books from the school and local libraries. Discard those tatty, grubby, books usually found in classroom library shelves, because they won't attract any little child to reading.

- Let children know that you will write for them at any time. You will write under a painting or put a sign next to a building. Always encourage the children to try to write their captions or signs in their own way, before you actually write them. It is wise to have a collection of long strips of paper readily available.

- Praise highly any child's attempts at writing, even if you cannot read it. For a young child, an early attempt at writing may be a wavy line.
- Inform children that if they bring books from home you will read them to the class.
- Have meaningful signs displayed at eye level around the classroom. Some of these signs will be changed regularly, for example by the sand tray.

You may add water to the sand to-day.

Come to the teacher's table to collect cars for the sand.

There are scone cutters to use in the sand this week.

- Start a school post office. All you need is a red painted post box and a grade of children who will take responsibility for clearing the box and delivering the letters. If the children cannot write for themselves they can post their drawings to their friends or ask their teacher to write their letters for them.

Helen St. Post Office

This letter box is cleared daily at 2.00pm.

Address your letters like this.

Mark Jones Room 9.

- Make experience books about things the children do at school. The children can illustrate these books or incorporate photographs in them.
- Take photos of the children and write about them. Always write what the child wants written, that is what the child says.

- Take photos of the children and write about them.

- Have a daily news sentence displayed first thing each morning, for example

We go to the library to-day.

or

It's Maria's birthday to-day.

NOT

To-day is Monday. It is cold and wet.

How monotonous it must become for children to have to copy a sentence about the day and weather on every morning of the school year.
- Let children know that reading can be fun. Set up a riddle display in your classroom or in a corridor. Children should be encouraged to add riddles to the display.

What did one ghost say to the other ghost? Gareth.

don't spook until you're spooken to.

(The answer is under a flap.)

- Have paper of various shapes, sizes and colours for the children to write and draw upon.
- Have various types of crayons, felt pens and pencils available for the children's use. Writing can become tedious if it is always done on rectangular pieces of white paper with black pencils.
- Let children write on a variety of surfaces, such as foam rubber, bark, silver paper, corrugated cardboard, calico and cellophane.
- Try to have a couple of old typewriters which are in working order in your classroom. Let the children experiment with them and try to type their work on them.
- Perhaps your school will buy a large print typewriter. A parent may volunteer to type the children's work to make a book.

SUMMARY

Before children can be expected to learn to read and write they have first to know what reading and writing are. As well, they have to appreciate that there is value for them in learning to read and write. The teacher's task is to motivate children so that they are excited by reading and writing, so that they see purpose for them in learning to read and write, so that they want to learn to read and write. As well, the teacher of beginner children must be able to identify those children who are ready to read and write on school entry.

When you SMILE everyone sees your teeth

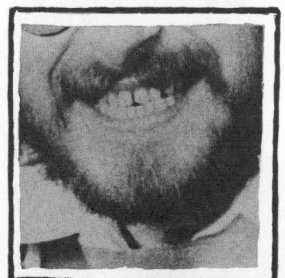 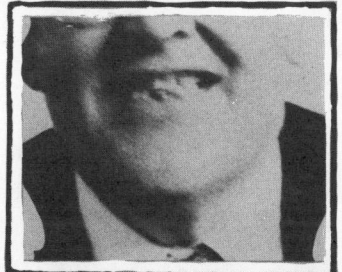 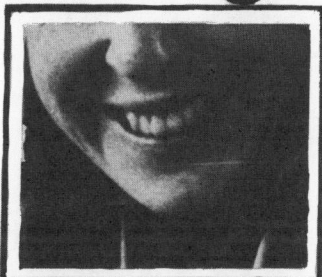 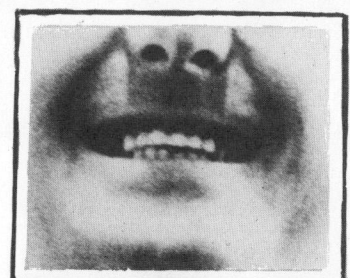

Match the teeth with the smiles.

About the language experience approach

Definition

Simply, the language experience approach described in this book is an approach for developing children's language (listening, speaking, reading and writing), out of their first-hand experiences. Implicit in this definition is the development of thought. At the same time as children's language grows out of their experiences, children use their language to make sense of their experiences.

This approach should not be confused with some published language experience readers or kits. These kits and readers are so named because through them children are given experience with language, almost invariably with someone else's written language. Such language has not arisen from the child's personal experiences. Hence this is a vastly different approach from developing children's language from their personal experiences; that is, those things children do and are part of.

Language Experience: An approach for children of all ages

The language experience approach can be used to develop children's language throughout the whole school. It is sometimes said that this approach is intended as an initial literacy or initial reading programme. It is much more than that. It is a splendid way to continue developing children's language long after they are reading and writing. Then, teachers can continue to use children's personal experiences to develop further their abilities in listening, speaking, reading and writing and reasoning. Of course, once children are writing they become their own scribes and once thay are reading they move on to published materials. Here, through experiencing someone else's language, they learn more about language and through reading about someone else's experiences, they can reflect upon their own, possibly challenge existing ideas and so accommodate new understandings.

You may well be asking, but why language experience? How can we teachers justify the use of children's experiences to develop their language? I will try to answer those questions in this chapter by discussing five separate issues.

1 OUR LANGUAGE IS THE PRODUCT OF OUR EXPERIENCES

Each one of us is the product of our experiences. Your view of the world will differ from mine because we've been in different places and done different things. I have a particular view of policemen because my father was a policeman all his working life. My view of the police force differs greatly from the view held by the Northcote children. It was a new experience for me, during my first year at Northcote, to see the children's reactions when the local constables visited the school. The children would scatter across the yard to the whispered 'Fuzz! Fuzz!' And a more specific recollection . . . During my first term at the school, the police courtesy squad visited to address the children on road safety, 'stranger danger' and other related matters. We assembled the three hundred infants in the school hall. When the policemen and policewomen entered the hall, one five-year-old boy took off. He could not be induced to come out from under a table in his classroom until the police officers had left the building. That five-year-old boy's view of police officers differed from mine. His life experiences relating to policemen had differed from mine. Postman and Weingartner (1972) say

> Our perceptions come from us . . . since our perceptions come from us and our past experiences, it is obvious each individual will perceive what is out there in a unique way.

> . . . meaning is not in words. Meaning is in people, and whatever meaning words have are assigned to them by people.

Each one of us is a product of our life experiences and from our experiences has grown our language. Britton (1970) has worded it this way

> Events take place and are gone: it is the representation that lasts and accumulates and undergoes successive modification.

Of course language is one way of representing experience. Strickland (1970) says

> The child's language is a product of his life experience. He learned what he had opportunity to learn —what was there for him . . .

The Need for Continuing Experience

What then are the implications for school practice? If a child's language is to continue to expand he must continue to experience. His vocabulary will be determined by his experiences. It is important for teachers to carefully select and plan experiences that are appropriate for their students; experiences which will engage their attention and which they can assimilate. As well, since a child and his language are the products of his experience, the school should not ignore his pre-school and out-of-school experiences.

2 LANGUAGE IS CENTRAL TO LEARNING

Language is one way of representing experience. Our language is what we know or understand on any given subject. We constantly change our representation of the world as a result of continued experience and the sharing of ideas with others. Language is more than communication, for as we speak, so we learn: as we speak we are adding to and modifying our representation of the world. Barnes (1976) says

> The importance of language and other symbolic systems such as mathematics is that it makes knowledge and thought processes readily available to introspection and revision. If we know what we know then we can change it. Language is not the

same as thought, but it allows us to reflect upon our thoughts.

I said earlier, as we speak so we learn. Similarly, as we write so we learn, for by writing we are able to bare our thoughts and so reflect upon them. In the following piece of writing, a ten-year-old boy reflects upon the death of his father, six months after the actual event. He and his classmates were asked to write about the topic 'Myself'.

> "Myself".
>
> Myself I have a lot of freckles. My eyes are brown I am pretty tall. My friends are Russell and John and Mario, Robert, Asan, Joe, Darren, Nicholas my best friend lives in Thomastown he is Johnie R. I have two sisters a mother. My father died on the 4/7/75 he was a good man he died of cancer and fluid I loved him. He was a butcher in Preston he was beired at faukner century I visit him but I am not going to visit him much because I get upset I miss him I loved him more than God and Jesus I didn't see when he died I only seen 5 weeks before he died when I visted him I thought he would live but he didn't he was 48 in age I always think about him Sometimes the cloud look like his face. I wish I could of kissed him before he passed on. My father always took me everywhere. My friends are Michael Smith and Jamie. I am not Michael's friend because he swears too much I am not Jamie's friend because he called my father names I will never be there friend unless they bring my father back to live.

A ten-year-old boy uses writing to express his thoughts about a personal experience. His language reflects his understanding of his father's death at the time of writing. His changes of tense show his difficulty in accepting that his father is no longer with the family. Note, 'I love my father I love him him very much I wish I could of kissed him before he passed on'.

Language is Central to Learning in All Areas of the Curriculum

Language is central to learning, be the subject mathematics, health, science or any other. In any of these subjects the particular body of knowledge is represented by language. Children's language will reveal their understanding of the subject. As well, through using language children will challenge and modify existing understandings in those subjects. Language is central to learning in any area of the curriculum and so children are encouraged to describe new concepts and new processes in their own language. For example, in mathematics children now speak and write about addition, or the joining of groups, in their own individual ways when they are first learning that process. After a child has manipulated four bottle tops with three bottle tops to make one group of seven bottle tops, he is asked to tell about what he has done. He might say,

> Four bottle tops and three bottle tops make seven bottle tops.

or

> I joined four tops with three tops and now I have seven.

The more precise mathematical terms 'plus' and 'equal' are introduced only when the child is fully confident as to what happens when groups are joined together. The child's own language reveals his understanding of the process.

3 CHILDREN LEARN LANGUAGE BY USING IT

Children learn to talk by talking. Linguists have shown how language acquisition is not just imitation of what adults say. Young children generate sentences which they could never have heard spoken by anybody else. It is now thought that language acquisition is a process of hypothesis formulating and testing.

My four-year-old niece, Allison, visited me one school holiday and excitedly said to me as she came in the door.

Auntie, Auntie. Daddy buyed me a doll.

My sister looked horrified and said

Where does she get it from? Geoff and I don't say 'buyed'.

And they don't. Language learning is not a matter of imitating what a parent says. From listening to people speaking around her, Allison had hypothesised that for the past tense of a verb one added 'ed'. This is the case for many verbs (for example jumped, barked, hopped), but as we know there are irregular verb forms and 'buy' is one of these. So Allison had gleaned a rule from her listening environment and in her enthusiasm she overapplied that rule: 'buy' 'buyed'.

Twelve months later when she was five years old, Allison again visited me during the vacation. This time as she ran in the door she called out

Auntie, Auntie. I writ you a letter. Did you get it?

Here she is experimenting with another form of the past tense which she has quite logically hypothesised from the language she has heard

bite, bit
light, lit
write, writ

As children learn to talk by talking so children learn to write by writing. The process the child is following is the same as for oral language acquisition, that is he is formulating hypotheses about language and testing them.

Stages of Development in Children Coming to Write for Themselves

1   The scribble stage.

Here the child has hypothesised that one sends messages to someone else by putting squiggly marks on paper. The starting point may be anywhere on the page.

Here the line is continuous, but the child has started at the side of the page and moved from left to right across it. He has hypothesised that one sends a message to someone else by putting squiggly marks on paper and also that when writing a message one starts at the left hand side of the paper and proceeds straight across.

2 Personal or non-conventional symbols.

John, 5 years

Here the child separates the squiggles or non-conventional symbols and obeys the directional features of our written language. This writing is seen frequently in beginner or first year intake classrooms. It is here for the first time for many children that they are introduced to script print, not long hand or linked writing. John has hypothesised that one sends messages to someone else by putting squiggles on paper, that one writes from left to right across the page and that writing is a collection of separate symbols.

All the rain is coming down.

Effie, 5 years

With her personal or non-conventional symbols Effie included several conventional letters from the alphabet. Effie read back her writing as

All the rain is coming down.

THE LANGUAGE EXPERIENCE APPROACH 15

3 Strings of conventional symbols.

Here the child strings together many letters from the alphabet and moves from left to right across the page and progressively down.

> DifetheL DIEImietlieeJieiSD. iSth
> DDthetDIeyOC bpqrwZsiwisDjSth
>
> Linda, 6 years

Linda read this as describing the pieces of string which she had joined together to measure the room. The child in this stage of development in writing has hypothesised that when people write they use a particular set of symbols and these symbols are repeated again and again, that is people don't invent their own symbols.

> Wi PSII 7HK Lola
> AGTn DPY m gt.
> Bq tV enc
> Sue and Pauline and
> Mrs Andrews are
> sitting on the mat.
>
> Lola, 5 years

4 Groups of letters with spaces between each group.

Here there is no match between the letters used and the sounds of the words, but the child has some concept of a word.

Notice how the teacher has written for Lola, what Lola herself wrote in her personal code.

5 Writing where the child reveals his developing awareness of sound-symbol correspondences.

> 19/11   Marie
> mi   mpmi   KPm
> with   mE to   thA
> MUZEAM.

(My mummy came with me to the museum.)

Here any person who is literate in English is able to read back what the child has written.

There may be children entering beginning classes who will be at any one of these stages of development in writing. Teachers will observe and praise. The child who is scribbling is starting to write. How exciting! The teacher will see the stage of development the child is at and incidentally mention something about written language which she thinks appropriate to the child's understanding. For example, Linda's teacher showed her a page of print from a picture story book. She asked Linda to touch individual words and then showed her the spaces between the words.

Linguists tell us that children's oral language acquisition is a series of rule making or hypothesis formulating and testing. In the right environment young children's development in writing follows the same process: hypothesis formulating and testing.

As mentioned earlier, as the child progresses through the stages described above, the teacher sometimes takes the opportunity to write the child's utterance for him. This ensures that the child continually sees the conventional written form of our language. The child may copy beneath the teacher's transcription.

My dad had a smash yesterday.
My dad had a smash yesterday.

The premise is that *children learn language by using it*. Children learn to talk by talking; children learn to write by writing. It can be argued that all children's language occurs on two levels.

1 The level of meaning: what he has to say or deep structure.

2 The level of language usage: how he says it or surface structure.

Surface Structure and Deep Structure of Language

I refer now to the surface and deep structure of language. Surface structure is the physical form of language as the eye sees it or as the ear hears it. It is to do with individual words, the length of utterances and, in written language, spelling and punctuation. Deep structure is to do with the underlying meaning of the passage. (Smith, 1971.)

Children's communication occurs on two levels and adults respond to each of these levels.

1 We comment on the meaning or deep structure, and so indicate that communication has taken place.
2 We provide feedback about the child's use of language or surface structure. In speech

Toddler Mummy come.
Adult Yes, Mummy is coming in the door.

The adult indicates that he understands the child's communication as well as showing him an expanded form of his utterance.

As in speech so in writing. Children must feel free to use writing, as well as speech, to convey meaning. In the example below an eight-year-old feels free enough with his limited written surface structure to convey what he feels.

Here is a man.
Here is a girl.
This is a boy.
This is a house.

To Overly Concern Children with Surface Structure in Both Speaking and Writing Can Impede their Efforts to Convey Deep Structure

Teachers who insist on correct spelling, sentence form and punctuation in children's writing, may prevent those children from using writing to convey meaning. By such practice, teachers can impede children from using writing to clarify their thinking. In some infant schools the following kind of sentence is seen frequently either written by teachers under the children's drawings or written by the children themselves.

I feel the frequency of use of this type of sentence form by young children is the result of the following practices:

1. The teacher insists that she write something under a child's drawing. Sometimes the drawing has conveyed all the meaning that the child intended. To please the teacher the child gives a very simple sentence.
2. The child gives a one-word or two-word utterance about his drawing and the teacher insists that the child expand the utterance into a sentence.
3. When a child will not give an utterance about a drawing the teacher uses her surface structure to frame the meaning that she thinks the child intended.
4. Where a child can write for himself but his teacher pays more attention to aspects of surface structure than to the intended meaning, the child here resorts to writing something *safe*, that is something he can spell correctly. Contrast these short stilted sentences with the writing of Helen aged eight years. She voluntarily produced this piece of writing after she upset her teacher one day.

Me and Stefany was noty wen the other chilldren was worcking and this is wot we did. We sat in The libbry conar and we wear pretending That we wor riding (Ed.-reading) and Then Miss Kave sade to us dont play but we dident lisen and Miss Kave told us abat 5 times to dont play and Then she sed to us you will have no free play.

This example illustrates that Helen does not feel so restricted by aspects of surface structure that she cannot use writing to freely express her thoughts. Incidentally, Helen is a Greek pupil who spoke very little English when she started school. Helen's teacher would respond appropriately if she talked with her about her behaviour, and how she felt about missing free play and, on the level of usage, perhaps discuss with her the use of capital letters.

The implications for school practice of the knowledge that children learn language by using it are that classrooms should offer children many opportunities to write and talk, and that teachers should provide feedback to the two levels of language.

4 ALL CHILDREN ARE DIFFERENT

We know that all children are different. They vary in physical, emotional, social and intellectual competence. We know that their life experiences and their language environments will have differed. Children's vocabulary reflects their experiences while their usage reflects the language they will have heard around them.

Jodi is in her first year at school. Can we tell anything about her language environment from this sample of her language?

A old man haven't got nobody to mind with.

Jodie C.

THE LANGUAGE EXPERIENCE APPROACH 19

Helen Street School.
Where is Helen St. School.
I asked the road
    but it wouldn't tell.
I asked the sign-post
but it just went on pointing.
So then I asked the
Govement but they just
said go away this is
no place for young
children to play.
At last tired and nearly
asleep I just caught
a glance of a child
running past.
I tried to get the
child to stop but alas
I fell asleep.
But I am going to
keep on searching
for the long lost school.
The school named
Helen Street School.

Natalie transferred into our school during her grade 3 year. She wrote easily and frequently in the poetic mode. The sample included here was the first piece of writing that she did at Helen Street. We remarked to her mother about Natalie's interest in writing and we learned that Natalie's grandfather and aunt had each published poetry. Natalie's use of language tells much about her family's interest in language.

The language experience approach, in which children's language is developed from their experiences, enables the teacher to incorporate individual differences into the learning programme, for the programme begins with the child: with his language and his experiences.

Because children are so different we cannot justify setting standards according to age. Think of the differences there will be in the confidence, vocabulary, language usage and attitudes towards learning to read and write, of first-year children. The teacher's task is to set appropriate goals for each child that take account of his previous performance and to plan programmes to achieve those goals.

Once we plan for individual difference and not for an age norm we write failure out of the curriculum.

5 THERE ARE INTERRELATIONSHIPS BETWEEN LISTENING, SPEAKING, READING AND WRITING

The four language areas which we aim to develop in school are listening, speaking, reading and writing. Their growth is inter-related, for example, children will not read until they have some competence with oral language.

Listening and speaking are to do with oral language; reading and writing are to do with written language.

Listening and reading are both ways of receiving language, speaking and writing are ways of expressing language.

These are the more obvious relationships. I will spend some time now looking at the relationship between speaking and reading.

> Reading involves the processing of three types of information. They are grapho-phonic, semantic and syntactic. (Goodman, 1973.)

Reading is not looking closely at all the print on the page. The reader takes a sample of print and then predicts according to syntactic knowledge (that is the reader's understanding of grammar) and semantic knowledge (that is the reader's experiental understanding of the topic he is reading). This will be demonstrated as you read the following passage.

Bozo the Clown

'Bozo' said . . . Circus Boss, 'We've lost . . . lion tamer. You'll have . . . take his place'. 'But . . . ', said Bozo with a . . . , 'I'm no lion tamer! . . . just a plain clown'. . . . now a lion tamer', . . . Boss said as he . . . away. 'Be ready for . . . act in an hour'. ' . . . my! What are you . . . to do Bozo? asked . . . his little friend. Bozo . . . for a minute. 'Follow . . . into my dressing tent', . . . said. 'I think I've . . . an idea and you . . . help.' (Buettner, 1962.)

You were able to read this quite easily because, after taking a visual sample, you predicted and supplied the missing words, aided by your knowledge of grammar and of the subject matter.

Because we are predicting when we read we sometimes change the text to language with which we are more comfortable. The children at Northcote read from *The Three Little Pigs*. The text ran

Once upon a time there were three little pigs . . .

Each child reading to me read

Once upon a time there was three little pigs . . .

They were predicting according to their own language usage. It then becomes clear that all oral reading errors or miscues are not bad.

With a language experience approach a child's first reading materials are his utterances written for him by his teacher. It then becomes possible for the child to draw upon all three sources of information to get meaning. That is, he not only processes information from the print or visual source, but he also uses non-visual information, that is he draws upon his experiences for semantic information and his knowledge of grammar for syntactic information.

Me and my sister.

Chris' teacher has written his utterance exactly as he spoke it. Chris is not yet reading but, when he later tries to read the print, he will guess or predict by drawing upon his own semantics and syntax. Because the language is his own there will be some chance of Chris forming a match between the written and the spoken word.

Many published early reading materials work against the reading process for they force the child to rely solely on the print. How can a child predict with the following text? How can he draw upon experiential and syntactic information?

Work.
Work, Dick.
Work, work.
See, see.
See Dick Work. (The Happy Trio 'Reading Scheme'.)

This is not the language of children. Such published materials deny the relationship between speaking and reading, for **how we speak, so we predict in reading.**

Perceptual Training

Reading is a language activity and therefore any early reading activities (readiness/pre-reading) must involve language. It has been shown that perceptual training activities which are not related to language do not contribute to learning to read. Examples of visual matching exercises which use language follow.

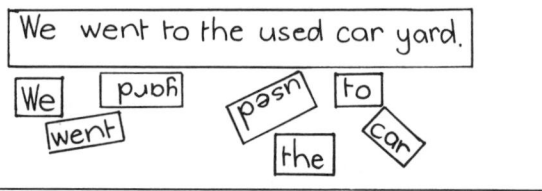

The child is asked to find his name which is written on a flash card, in other notices around the room.

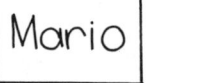

An auditory activity involving language is: After saying together *Humpty Dumpty* the teacher asks

What is the same about 'wall' and 'fall'?
What other words sound like 'wall' and 'fall'?

LANGUAGE EXPERIENCE APPROACH: Structured or unstructured

It is often said of the language experience approach that it is without structure. Possibly this criticism is made because no commercial materials are used, and the order of introduction of the specifics (for example letter identification, word identification) cannot be given before the programme is started.

I contend that the language experience approach as described in this book is more highly structured in practice than any published programme. Not only is it more highly structured, but the structure is more complex. It is within the teacher and consists of her knowledge of child development, of language acquisition and development, of the children in her class and, more specifically, of the reading process, incorporating a set of objectives for development in writing and reading. (Refer to page 77 for suggested objectives.) The teacher's task then becomes to match her knowledge about child development and language with her knowledge about her children, so she can estimate their stages of development and plan programmes accordingly. The learning programme will vary for each child: the experiences of each will be different, the written materials read by each child will be different, the order of word, sound and letter recognition will be different. How much simpler is the structure in most published reading schemes, in which each child uses the same materials in the same order and may begin at the same starting place.

I contend again: the language experience approach is a highly structured approach to developing children's language and bringing children to literacy.

SUMMARY

Because

1. Our language is the product of our experiences
2. Language is central to learning
3. Children learn language by using it
4. All children are different
5. Listening, speaking, reading and writing are interrelated in development;

so a language experience approach is justified for the development of children's language. As well, the language experience approach is not unstructured. Instead of the structure being written into a set of materials, it is within the teacher.

Mr Jones has seven big fish.

3 About oral language

The major purpose of this book is to describe a language experience approach to literacy. Therefore, most of the book deals with reading and writing. However a language experience approach is designed to develop all areas of a child's language: listening, speaking, reading and writing.

Reading is a language activity and hence much time must be devoted to developing children's spoken language during their years at primary school. As we saw above, children's language development is a process of rule formulating and testing. Children listen to people speaking around them, extrapolate rules about usage and then practise them. Hence children learn to talk by talking and therefore children's talk should be encouraged in school.

Directed Discussion

There are two main categories of oral language in which children will be engaged during school time. They are directed discussion and spontaneous chatter. During the directed discussion or directed oral activity, the concern is with exploring a particular idea or topic. The directed discussion may be between the teacher and the whole class; the teacher and a small group of children; the teacher and an individual child; a small group of children without a teacher. In each case there is a particular task or topic to discuss.

Spontaneous Chatter

Children's spontaneous chatter may change direction as the interests or impulses of the participants determine. It will occur during their daily activities such as walking to school, building with blocks, doing puzzles or making pictures. It is natural for little children to talk as they work or play and the school should encourage this talk, not discourage it.

I'm going to Greece. My grandma is there and my cousins.
It's nice at Greece. Maria and Patricia went to Greece for a holiday.

Oral chatter in the classroom from a six-year-old Greek girl.

I said. 'Dad do you want a lolly', but I hid them somewhere. He got the box but there was nothing there. I got smacked across my face.

From a six-year-old Jugoslav boy to his teacher.

EXPRESSIVE SPEECH

Not only is it natural for little children to talk, it is very important that they do. In their continuing efforts to learn about the world, children need to experience at first-hand, and time and opportunity to recreate their experiences. In trying to sort out reality, children play, model, draw, write and talk about what happens to them. All these are ways in which we can represent experience. My sister-in-law was greeted by her son's kindergarten teacher one morning

> Mrs Wilson, do you by any chance frequently rearrange the furniture in your home?

My sister-in-law gave an embarassed laugh and asked

> How do you know?

The kindergarten teacher replied

> I have never seen a four-year-old child play for so long in the doll's corner, moving the furniture so frequently.

Terry, my nephew, was creating reality for himself through the medium of play, and in so doing was trying to understand his mother's behaviour.

A grade 1 teacher related this story to me about a six-year-old who attended a funeral with his family. The following morning he constantly approached his teacher with comments about the experience. He didn't wait for the teacher's reply, but simply uttered his remark and then went back to work. Some of his utterances were

> I went to the funeral.
> There were flowers on the coffin.
> Mummy was crying.
> The hole was six feet **deep**.

A six-year-old was clarifying reality for himself through talk. He was talking to understand.

Relationship between Expressive Activities

Teachers should be aware of children's need to express experiences. They must acknowledge the link between children's play, talk and painting and their thought development. By moving the doll's furniture around, Terry was sorting out his ideas about what his mother did at home. By talking about the funeral —recreating the experience through talk—the six-year-old boy was clarifying his thinking about death and funerals.

A school curriculum which aims to develop children's thinking will value talk, play, painting, drama, and other expressive activities. For, once one acknowledges the need for children to recreate reality, one will put a variety of media at their disposal. Not all children or all people are at ease with all media. Once I heard an artist who was addressing a group of teachers begin

> I hate standing here talking to you, for I consider myself a non-verbal person. When I have something of importance to say I say it with paint. A painting for me is the culmination of much deep thought.

In many schools the expressive activity which children are most often asked to do is writing. Writing is a far more difficult medium for children to use than talk or paint or play, and yet how often do we hear children say

> Whenever we go on an excursion we have to write about it.

Or at the end of the holidays

> Tomorrow we'll have to write about what we did over the holidays.

When schools only allow children to express themselves through writing they are restricting opportunities for many children to clarify their thinking, to sort out their ideas about the world. If children need to relive an experience they must feel at ease with the medium they use. Some people are more at ease with a particular medium than others. Artists obviously feel at ease with paints and oils, while dancers feel best when using their bodies to express what they have to say. In some situations one medium may be more appropriate than another. Marshall (1963) in *An Experiment in Education* describes an occasion when she asked an older pupil to paint her family. The girl spent some time trying to paint her family and then said to Sybil Marshall

> I could write about my family better than I could paint it.

The girl wrote a lengthy piece about the many family members. For that girl at that time writing was the medium most suited to her needs.

Talk, then, is a medium we use to review reality. For young children it is an easy medium. I have spent some time describing the expressive nature of children's talk. Of course children's talk has other very important functions: to socialise, to seek information, to give information, to direct or regulate the behaviour of others.

COMPONENTS OF AN ORAL LANGUAGE PROGRAMME

The following are the key ingredients of a programme which is designed to stimulate and develop children's talk

1. a warm accepting atmosphere
2. high-quality adult interaction
3. a physical environment which facilitates and stimulates children's talk
4. learning experiences which stimulate talk.

A Warm Accepting Atmosphere

Teachers need to see the relationship between children's chatter and their learning about language; between children's talk and the development of their intellect. Children's talk must be valued. When teachers value children's language, they will encourage children's talk in the classroom. All children should feel that their talk is welcomed and that no child's language is considered inferior.

High-Quality Adult Interaction

A good learning environment, in which the child experiences both in and out of the classroom, will stimulate talk. However, to extend his language, a child needs to talk with adults and other children who have more highly developed language. When talking with children, teachers should use certain strategies to extend children's language. When a child speaks, he is firstly trying to get a message across and secondly trying out his language. The adult, in responding to the child's utterance, should show that he has understood the message, and provide feedback about **the language the child has used.** For example

Child Daddy buyed me a car.
Adult Aren't you lucky. Your daddy bought you a toy car.
Child Mummy gone.
Adult Yes. Mummy's gone to get the milk.

Notice how the adult expands or elaborates the child's language while indicating that she understands what the child says.

Questioning technique is a most important part of an adult's oral interaction with children. Many educationists have outlined hierarchies of questions, all of which begin with closed questions and progress to open questions. A simple one is outlined at right.

It is possible that some teachers are not aware of a hierarchy of questions and of their own dependence on closed questions, that is questions which have specific right answers. For example

What colour is the roof?

The skill of asking questions which require divergent thinking, or the recognition of relationships is one which most people have to learn. Before discussing something with children, teachers should plan some questions they might ask. All teachers could make frequent use of questions which begin

What would happen if . . .
Why is it so . . .
How is a . . . like a . . .
Why did you say that?
Explain what you mean.
What do you think about that?

Purpose of question	Example
To request information	What is that?
To request greater accuracy of information.	What colour is it? From what is it made?
To request explanation.	How did you make that?
To request prediction.	What would happen if you added more sugar to the mixture?
To request similarities and differences.	How is the car like the truck? How is the car different from the truck?
To request synthesis.	From the graph we have made about the members of our families, what can you tell about our families? For example, some families are bigger than other families; all of our families are different.
To request judgement.	How would you rate the action taken by the leader?
To request reasoning.	Why is it that more cars pass our school between 12.00 and 1.00 pm than at any other time of the day?

Of course questions requiring factual answers have to be asked. Before asking children to comment upon similarities and differences, for example, a teacher needs to know if they understand the necessary facts. In a discussion on transport a teacher may want children to work out the similarities and differences between road and rail transport. Before expecting children to do this she should check to see if the children have the necessary understanding of both road and rail transport by asking questions such as:

What is a road train?
Describe a semi-trailer?
Who operates the railway system?

A Physical Environment which facilitates and Stimulates Children's Talk

All primary-school classrooms should be stimulating places to enter, with much equipment suitable for children of that age. The building area in the infants' classroom will contain large building blocks, while in the upper primary room it will have much smaller, interlocking materials. The games area for infants might house dominoes and snap; for older children, chess and scrabble. Large wooden jigsaws are suited to young children, small intricate ones hold challenge for older pupils.

It is important for all primary-school children, to have a wide variety of materials to handle, but it is crucial for migrant pupils who speak little or no English. Sand, construction materials, art media, cassette players are universal learning materials and can challenge and stimulate new understandings in a child of any nationality. To let migrant children with little English sit quietly through the day while the teacher talks is to waste precious time.

Once teachers have materials like those listed above they need to ensure that their classroom arrangement allows maximum use of the materials. As well, room arrangement should encourage children to talk, work and play with each other. For this to work smoothly and profitably, the order in a room must be evident to the children. Each area (for example writing area, building area,) must be clearly defined and its particular rules understood by the children.

Some Useful Hints in Room Arrangements
• Each piece of equipment should belong in a set place. The teacher should label as many home positions as possible.

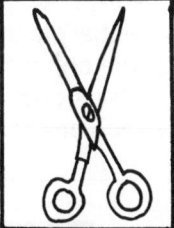

A picture can show where some equipment is stored.

If everything is kept in a set place it is much easier to check whether any equipment is missing at the end of each day.
• Equipment should be kept at child height so that children can collect and return it by themselves.
• It is sometimes a good idea to remove cupboard doors for easy collection of materials and quick checking of equipment.
• If children continually leave an area untidy, your organisation may be at fault. If the dressup clothes are always on the floor, it might be because there are

not enough hooks and hangers. Or perhaps the hooks are too high for the children to reach.
- Avoid having the building area in a thoroughfare.
- Avoid having the sand tray next to the water tray, or you might end up with two trays of mud.
- Try to have the water tray near the door to avoid carrying water through the room. If the room has a tap, place the water tray near it.
- Do have an established quiet area where the children can sit to read and write.
- See which materials the children do not use. Try to find out why the equipment is ignored. Is it in an out-of-the-way position? Do the children know its potential? Is the equipment too difficult or too simple for the children in the class?
- Use signs to indicate how many children can work in each area.

> 6 children in the building area.

> Only 2 children use the cassette player.

A Suggested Room Arrangement

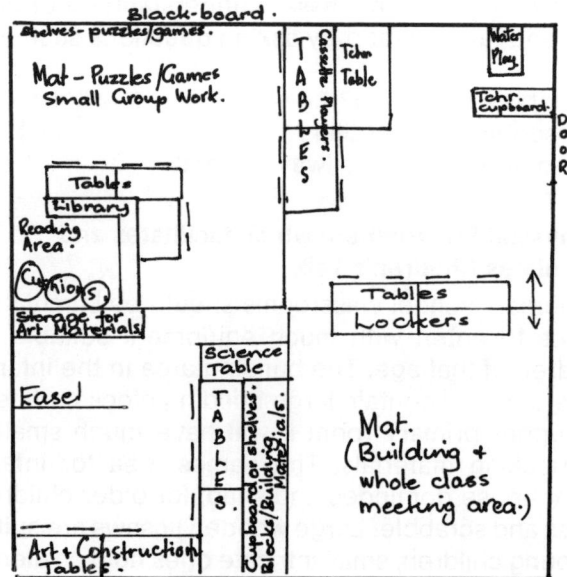

Learning Experiences which Stimulate Talk

First-hand experiences include all those things which happen to children; all the activities in which they take part. A fight with another child is a first-hand experience for the children involved, as is cleaning a pet's cage in the classroom. First-hand experiences happen in the classroom, in the school yard, in the neighbourhood, in the wider community and at the child's home. First-hand experiences do not only happen on excursions. Most of a very young child's school learning experiences occur in the classroom.

The richness of these experiences depends on what kinds of equipment and activities the teacher offers. For further ideas see Chapter 4.

If there are, in a child's classroom, materials to use, people to talk with and an environment where talk is welcomed, he will talk. In such conditions there is no need to contrive oral language games in fixed oral language periods. Many oral language games focus only upon the surface structure of language and divorce it from the deep structure. An example of this type of oral language activity is the *Shopping Game*. The purpose of this game is to teach children to use 'bought' rather than 'buyed'.

Child A   I went to the supermarket.
Child B   What did you buy?
Child A   I bought fish.
Child B   I went to the supermarket.
Child C   What did you buy?
Child B   I bought biscuits.
Child C   I went to . . .

Feedback about children's language usage should be given in a meaningful context. In this case, it might profitably occur during a visit to a supermarket, or in the classroom shop.

SUMMARY

Reading is a language activity and as such is dependent on the development of children's spoken language. To extend their language, children need to interact with people who use more highly developed language. Teachers need to know how to elaborate children's spoken language and how to use different kinds of questions. The classroom environment and learning programme should be such that they stimulate children to talk, and the atmosphere should be one in which children know their talk is valued.

4. About the experiences a teacher may draw upon to develop children's language

Experiences which stimulate children's language may come from many different sources.

TRADITIONAL SCHOOL SUBJECTS ARE RICH IN FIRST-HAND EXPERIENCES FOR CHILDREN

Alex, aged ten years, had come from Argentina six months before his grade went to the beach. From a science excursion came opportunities for development in language.

Barry, aged five years, in his first year at school remarked to his teacher that something was taller than a house. He could not think of any other things which could be taller than a house so his teacher directed Barry to take a little friend, go out into the schoolground and observe all the things that were taller than the houses in the street. When Barry and Suzanne returned to the classroom they drew everything that they now knew to be taller than houses. The drawings were stapled together into a book and the teacher wrote captions at the children's direction.

At the Beach
On Monday I went to the Beach whth my grade and I found a Shell with the animal in it and I opened and I took the animal out of the shell. The animal was very soft and little, the colour pink, and I took the shell home.
by Alex

All things that are taller than a house.
by Barry and Suzanne
Room 8

From mathematical experience arose a chance for children to learn more about reading and writing. As the teacher wrote for the children, she talked about what she was doing. She used technical terms such as 'word', 'capital letter', 'full stop'. She commented on the direction of the handwriting and of course they read back the writing about their experience.

A class of eight-year-olds went to visit a farm as part of their study of the environment. Afterwards, they compiled a graph depicting the most popular animal at the farm. They interpreted their findings and dictated them to their teacher who wrote under the graph.

My favourite animal or bird at the farm.

cow	bull	donkey	duck	dog	rooster	calf
	Jimmy					
	Bill	Adam				
		Michelle				
	Peter	Kathy	Tony			
	Con					
	Steve W	Stan	Tracy	Karen	Peter	
	John	Ross	Anna	Lucy	Helen	
Frans	Sam		Susie	Miss Kave	Chris	Nick
David	Andrew	Tim	Mike	Maria	Mileva	David

This is a graph about our favourite animal or bird at the farm. Con and Sam were in charge of the graph. The bull was the most popular. Thirteen people liked the bull. Ten people liked the donkey. Two people liked the cow. Five people liked the duck the best. Two people liked the dog the best. No-one liked the rooster and the calf. The rooster and the calf were the least popular. Two people liked the cow and the dog. Each square stands for one person. Thirty-two people worked on the graph.

Remember opportunities to develop children's language can arise from experiences in any subject.

EQUIPMENT WHICH ENRICHES THE CLASSROOM WILL BE A SOURCE OF EXPERIENCES FOR CHILDREN

Of course much oral language is developed when children are using materials. However, I want particularly to illustrate how children's writing and reading can grow out of their experiences, so again I will use a written example.

After building with the large kindergarten blocks three five-year-old boys wanted a sign attached to their finished building. They told the teacher what to write and of course she asked the children to read it back.

> Leonidis Kon and Pedro built this house and we have got guns and wheels.

EXPERIENCES WHICH GIVE RISE TO TALKING, LISTENING, READING AND WRITING CAN BE THINGS THAT HAPPEN ABOUT THE SCHOOL

Building alterations at the school provide many first-hand experiences for the pupils.

> We have builders at
> we have builders at
> school They are making
> School They are making
> new toilets.
> new toilets

The child has copied beneath the teacher's writing.

After a school medical service sister tested his vision and hearing, Glenn, aged six years, wrote:

> We had our ears twisdead and it didnt hert it wos good Roger sed it didnt hert and I had my ears chekd last. it mad a noys Leo wos sekend and som mor Grad ones cam in Miss Wilens offes it wos good After I had my ears cheked a nuther Grad one cam in ther wos Crag Roger Leo and me We wer Dun Bfor the gther Grad ones cam in

ACTIVITIES INITIATED BY TEACHERS CAN BE A SOURCE OF EXPERIENCE FOR STIMULATING LANGUAGE DEVELOPMENT

One November, the teachers at Helen Street organised a billy-cart race for the children. Children could either make their carts at home or at school. Big kids were seen helping little kids in pre-race preparations and the race day was a very happy occasion. The teachers took many photographs during the races and used them on following days.

Craig is an older pupil and able to write for himself. His writing reveals ways that his teacher could teach him more about written language. Perhaps she could help Craig to punctuate sentences. If Craig read his story aloud he would punctuate it by pausing at the end of each sentence. He already knows that a full stop indicates the end of a sentence, but he is not always sure just where a sentence ends.

After the billy-cart race a teacher wrote for a younger pupil:

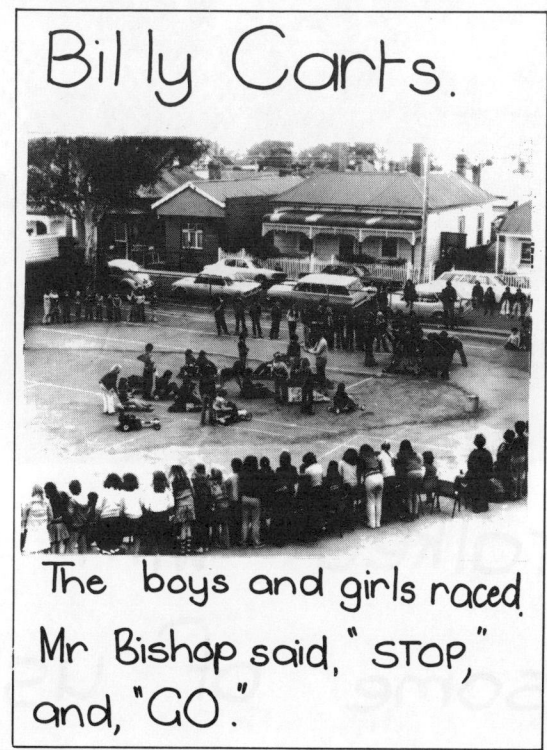

Photographs of the children and school events, together with the children's writing about the photos, should be constantly on display about the school, so that there are many opportunities for the children to read what others write.

WALKS IN THE NEIGHBOURHOOD PROVIDE WIDER EXPERIENCES

Children may be able to take cameras with them when they go out of the school. People of many

We met a greek grand mother who played and talked with us. She kissed some of us.

WRITE ME A SIGN

different nationalities live near the Helen Street school and the grandparents of the migrant children are often to be seen.

EXCURSIONS FURTHER AFIELD

Obviously excursions beyond the immediate school community are a rich source of experience.

Donny brook Springs.

On Tuesday The 14th we went to Donny brook. One of the girls in Mrs Scardon's Grade found an egg. The egg was cracked and Then Barry went to see the egg and he found a nest. The nest was 38 centimetres across. Then Barry showed the nest to the teachers. We had to eat our lunch. Some people had a barbecue. Some people ate in the huts. There where lots of Swings and a Soccer ground. Then Some people went to the mineral water. The best part I liked was going across The rocks, Some rocks were big and some rocks were small.

A CHILD'S HOME IS A SOURCE OF VARIED EXPERIENCES

The school day should be flexible enough to allow children to paint, draw, talk or build about home experience if they want to.

George was an unhappy six-year-old whose mother had left her family. His dog, Snoopy, was very dear to him. On two different days in June he asked his teacher to write for him.

My dog had pups and
My dog had pups and
I was watching the pups.
I was watching the pups
My dog named Snoopy.
My dog named Snoopy.

On the holidays and I
On the holidays and I
lost Snoopy. The council
lost shooppy The council
maybe got him. That's all.
maybe got him thots all.

EXPERIENCES TO DEVELOP CHILDREN'S LANGUAGE 43

SUMMARY

Experiences which give stimulus for language development can arise from the following sources.

1. The traditional subjects.
2. Classroom equipment such as dolls, blocks.
3. Everyday happenings about the school.
4. Activities initiated by teachers, such as hatching chickens, cooking.
5. Walks in the neighbourhood.
6. Excursions further afield.
7. Home experiences.

In all these types of experiences

1. Children learn about language by using it and
2. Children learn more about the experiences through using language.

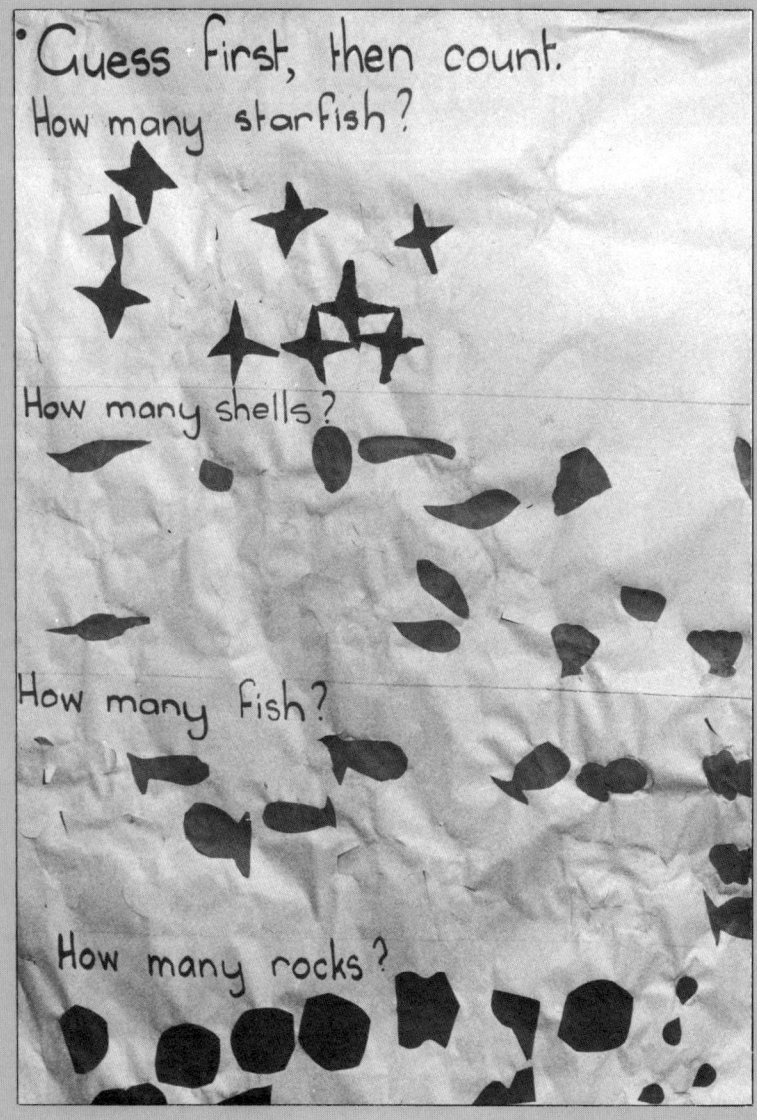

About classroom practice for teaching writing and reading from personal experience

Reading: The getting of meaning from print

One must look at just what reading is to fully appreciate how important it is to develop children's reading programmes from their personal experiences. Reading has been defined as the getting of meaning from print: it is not just a code cracking or word naming process. It is to do with meaning and hence involves thinking. Anyone of us can sound out unknown words with no idea of their meaning.

The extent to which the ideas of the reader will approximate to those intended by the author will depend on both the experiences of the reader and his linguistic competence. If there is no match between the experience described by the author and something the young reader has experienced, communication or understanding will not occur. If the language of the author is too sophisticated or too different from that which the reader can comprehend, again, no understanding may occur. For the beginning reader, how much simpler the reading task becomes when the message he reads is expressed in his own language and is about something which he has experienced. This can be achieved when the teacher writes a child's utterances for him. When a child reads back his utterance, he has the meaning within him and the language presents no difficulty for him because it is his own. The texts of many basal readers are without meaning.

> Look.
> Look, look.
> Oh, Oh, Oh.
> Oh, Oh.
> Oh, Look.

Tightly controlled vocabularies such as this make a mockery of reading for meaning. This text has been written to give practice in the recognition of individual words.

> This is the station. That's
> a train. It's a new train and
> it's fast too. There's a
> man. He's wearing a cap
> and a coat. There's a little
> boy. He's off to Sydney.
> There's a big boy. He's on
> the platform. Oh! He's
> taking that little boy's bag.
> He's a bad boy. (*Learning English in Australia*,
> Reader 18).

Again, the book has been written to practise a particular aspect of surface, structure, namely, contractions. Meaning has been given a lower priority.

Reading, the search for meaning or deep structure, becomes much simpler if what is read is about something which the child has experienced. It is simplified further if that experience has been recorded in the child's own language, for then there are no unfamiliar or difficult words or sentence patterns; that is no difficult surface structure to struggle with.

INDIVIDUAL OR GROUP TEACHING IN THE INITIAL LITERACY PROGRAMME

Individual or Group Organisation

Whether the initial literacy programme is interpreted in classroom organisation as an individualised informal approach or as a more formal programme depends on the teacher's experience and philosophy.

If the teacher is running an individualised activity room or an open classroom, she will obviously adopt an individualised approach. She will write utterances for individual children on sheets of paper, under paintings, by photographs, as signs for constructions.

In an individualised approach there may be no specific reading and writing time, as reading and writing will probably happen before the bell in the morning and at many different times during the day. However, even in the most free individualised classroom there will sometimes be a group or the whole class reading together. For example, when a new sign is displayed in the room and the teacher draws attention to it.

---

*This is a cassette player.
Two children may use it at the one time.
Could you make up a story and tell it into the cassette player.*

Or group reading may occur when a group of interested children work with the teacher in developing a wall story which has arisen from a shared experience. Some five-, six- and seven-year-olds from a multi-age room worked with their teacher to compile the following wall story about the birds they were keeping in their classroom. A wall story is not written directly on the wall but either on the chalkboard or a large sheet of paper.

---

*Our Birds.
The birds sing songs. To-day one of our birds died. One of our birds died yesterday. We have two birds left. The two canaries have died. Alex and Harry are going to look after the two budgies. The two budgies are alive. The two budgies eat bird seed. The two budgies whistle. Our budgies didn't die. These ones will die if they get sick. We like to look at the budgies because they are nice. If we separate the budgies they might die because they will be lonely. The end.*

When a wall story such as this is familiar to the children, it may be copied into a class experience book. As well, the teacher may duplicate smaller copies of the book, so that children have individual copies.

Large class experience book, which has the same text as the wall story.

Small duplicated books which have the same text as the wall story.

Sometimes too a group of children may read the same book and then meet to discuss it.

LANGUAGE EXPERIENCE WITH A GROUP

The following group approach is something of a compromise, because the sentence used is the utterance of only one child. However, the utterance arises from a shared experience.

At other times during the day the teacher will be writing for individual children. This may occur at free activity time or at art time for example. However, the following may be a useful teaching procedure for group work.

With a Group who are Non-Readers

These children will often have little understanding of the directional nature of our written language and of the technical terms.
- A shared experience; for example, the use of fingerpaint.
- Discussion.
- Teacher writes one child's sentence on the chalkboard.

The fingerpaint was cold.

Before she writes the sentence she says

If I start writing here, which way will I write across the chalkboard?

Several children would go to the chalkboard and show the direction of the writing. As the teacher writes she uses the technical terms 'word', 'capital', 'letter', 'sentence', 'full stop' and comments on the spacing between words.

She might say as she is writing

What is the first word in the sentence?
I start the sentence with a capital letter.
I'll leave a space after this word.
I put a full stop at the end of the sentence.

- Children read the sentence together.
- Individuals read the sentence.
- The teacher writes the sentence a second time. She again comments about the technical terms and, as well, she sounds each word as she writes it. The message she is getting across here is that words are made up of sounds.

'was' is sounded w o s
'paint' is sounded p ai n t (4 sounds)

- Children read the sentence.
- Individual children are asked to come to the chalkboard to touch a word. One child may be asked to touch and count the number of words in the sentence.
- The following day the teacher would have copies of the sentence prepared for the children to trace over and copy beneath.

The fingerpaint was cold.

- An indicator card of the sentence with an illustration drawn by a child is displayed at child height.

As well, the teacher prepares a sentence card and individual word cards so that children can match the sentence card with the sentences on the large story card. This language-matching is a very good pre-reading or readiness activity.
- A new sentence may be introduced to a group of children twice a week. Known sentences are revised regularly.

With a group of Children who Know the Directional Nature of Print, Know the Concepts 'Word', 'Letter', are Starting to Identify Words, and are Starting to Relate Sounds to Letters

- A shared experience. Examination of the classroom fishtank.
- Discussion.
- Teacher writes one child's sentence on the chalkboard.

One of our fish died.

As the teacher writes she asks

What is the first word in the sentence?
Which word will I write next?
What is the last word I need to write?

- Children read the sentence.
- Teacher writes the sentence again. This time she sounds each word as she writes it, and the children join in. She might ask

What is the next word?—fish.
What sound do you hear at the start of 'fish'?
- Children read sentence.
- Teacher asks individual children to find particular words.
John, come and touch the word 'fish.'
Who can find the word 'died'?

- She draws attention to particular letters.

Who can point to the letter representing the 'f' sound in fish?

- The teacher may draw attention to the number of sounds in particular words, for example

How many sounds are there in 'fish'?

If any of the children are able to copy the sentence direct from the chalkboard they may do so in a book, which is a collection of the group sentences.
- As in the previous lesson outlined, the teacher prepares a large indicator card, sentence card and word cards

Pocket for words.

- On the next day the teacher has copies of the sentence ready for the children to trace over and write beneath.
Another activity for children who are identifying the words in the sentence is to let them cut between

TEACHING LITERACY FROM PERSONAL EXPERIENCE

the words, mix them up, then re-arrange them into sentence order. The children then paste this sentence onto a second piece of paper.

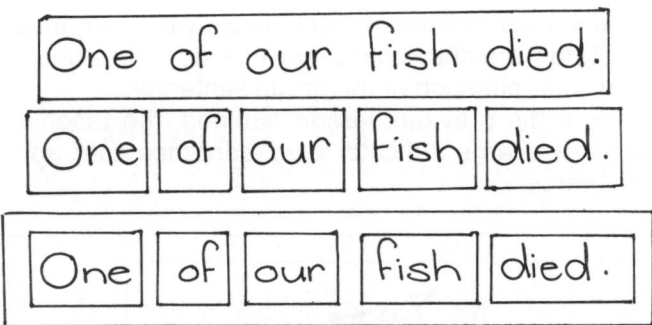

Children cut between words and mix them up.

The teacher may write a key interest word in large print on paper for children just beginning to identify words. The child can trace over the outline, then cover it with small pieces of torn paper. This activity should only be done on two or three occasions, as it is time consuming and can be very boring if done repeatedly.

• For children who are beginning to associate sounds and letters the teacher may write a letter which they noticed in the sentence, on a large piece of paper. Again the child traces over the outline and then covers it with small pieces of torn paper.

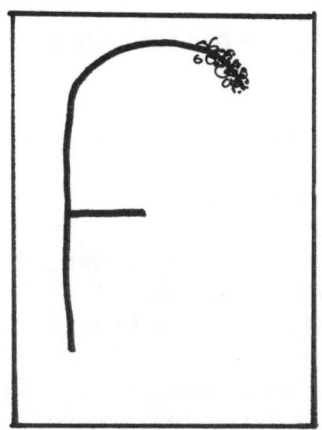

Or in a child's personal letter/sound book the teacher could enter 'f' on a new page. The child may copy words from around the room in which 'f' occurs, or draw pictures of items in which the child hears the 'f' sound.

• Teacher watches the children tracing and copying to see what practice they need in handwriting.

• Cut out the letter from sand-paper, velvet ribbon or any textured material. The letter is pasted on a large sheet of cardboard and displayed at child-height. The children can be encouraged to trace over the letter with their fingers.

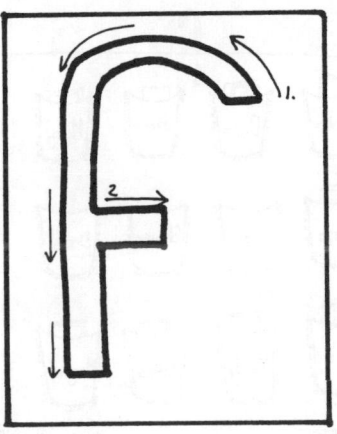

A letter made with velvet ribbon which the children may trace over with their fingers. Arrows show the direction to follow.

- Introduce a new sentence two or three times during the week. Read and revise known sentences regularly.
- When six class sentences have been treated in this way, duplicate and staple them into class reading booklets. Here each child illustrates his own little booklet, and then takes it home to read to his parents.

Personal Story Books

In any classroom, whether the teacher follows an individualised or group approach, the teacher will have personal story books prepared for the children to write or draw in at any time. If the teacher follows the group approach outlined above, she should ensure that the children do not only work in ability groups. For many language activities, children will be in friendship and mixed ability groups. When writing sentences in individual story books, the teacher could see that this group was a mixed ability group. Children learn language by talking with each other, not only to the teacher.

A teacher writing in one of these books would observe the following principles.

- Write exactly what the child says, whether it is a couple of words or a sentence, grammatically correct or not. Remember at this moment your concern is the teaching of reading. When the child reads back what you have written, you hope that he will make a match between the spoken and the written word. If you change his utterance to one which you consider more acceptable, the child will read it back as he said it originally and possibly form a mismatch between the written and the spoken word.

- Discuss the message with the child. Remember meaning is important.

- Make use of the technical vocabulary of our language, for example 'word', 'print', etc.
- Without undue emphasis, sound each word as you write it.
- According to the child's stage of literacy, ask him appropriate questions, for example

> How many words are there in the sentence?
> Put your hand on a word.
> Put your hand on the first word in the sentence.
> Point to a letter.
> Find the word that is 'father'.
> Find the letters that are making the 'sh' sound in 'shop'.

- As children come to identify individual words in their sentences, the teacher can write these words on cards which may then be stored in a pocket at the back of the book, or in a shoe tidy. If children have individual words on cards to handle, they can look closely at the words, compare them and try to combine them to create new sentences.

Many teachers think that a language experience approach is a totally individualised one. It can be a very individualised programme but I repeat that in all types of classrooms there are occasions for group reading, as when the children read a wall story prepared by one or several children. As well, in all types of classrooms there should be opportunities for individual children's utterances to be written for them. Some teachers think that a language experience approach is only for young children or only for beginning readers. As a beginning literacy method, the language experience approach is appropriate for someone of any age, that is infant or adult. The transcription of personal experience proves to be far more interesting reading material for older non-reading pupils than books written as infant readers.

TIMETABLING

Timetabling is a very personal matter for each teacher. By showing the way she organises her school day, her timetable is an expression of her philosophy about teaching. The timetable must take account of school policy and specialist subjects as well as shared special learning areas, for example the film room. Many teachers feel more secure in their teaching when they know exactly what they are teaching and when they are teaching it, while others have no fixed time slots for particular subjects. This latter group of teachers may follow an integrated curriculum and initiate input and output sessions for the children according to their needs and interests. For example, when the children are tired of a creative play session, the teachers will draw them together for a quieter time, perhaps a story, perhaps for musical appreciation. For teachers working an integrated day the only regularly timetabled periods may be those taken by specialist teachers (library, music) or in special teaching areas such as the gym or film room.

The timetable below is suggested for those teachers who prefer to know in advance when they will be teaching what subjects. Within each subject there is room for much flexibility. This timetable could be adapted for use from Beginners to Grade 6. Ideally the children enter the classroom one or two at a time, prior to the regulation school starting time. This means the teacher can personally greet each child each day. For an inexperienced teacher it is much easier to have the children entering individually or in twos and settling to an activity of their choice than to have thirty odd children marching in together: all pushing about their lockers at once. Of course this suggested organisation can only happen if there is no daily school assembly.

The current class theme could be the means of relating the activities in the various subject areas.

9:00AM	Free Activities.
	Morning Talk.
10:30AM	
10:45AM	Recess.
	Language Activities.
12:15PM	
1:15PM	Lunch.
	Maths.
2:15PM	
2:30PM	Recess.
	Art . Music . Phys-ed. Social Studies. Science . Health.
3:30PM	

Free Choice of Activities

At this time the children would use the classroom equipment such as the sand tray, puppets, book corner, art materials, felt board, puzzles, dress-up clothes, listening posts, typewriters, individual slide projectors, cassette players, etc. As well, the children may choose to continue small group projects or to complete writing or art begun the day before.

Morning Talk

Here the children will discuss home experiences and current affairs. As well, they discuss what they did during Free Choice of Activities time. Often, morning talk will be held in several small groups.

Language Activities

Here are several language activities for children of different ages. They could all be related to the current class theme or interest. (See below.)

Notice that in the upper school, cooking from a recipe and model making to directions are suggested as language activities. Not only do these activities stimulate much oral language but they require reading for a different purpose, that is reading for detail. We should ensure that children are required to read for different purposes, for example reading for the main idea, reading for detail, reading to skim. A teacher can have permanent cooking and model making areas in her classroom. One particular recipe and one set of directions, for example for making a kite, can be displayed until every child who is interested has had a turn at that activity.

Maths

Maths learning will occur, of course, at other times; for example when the children use the scales or blocks in Free Choice of Activities.

Art, Music, Physical Education, Health, Social Studies, Science

Again, learning in these subjects will occur at other times. If, for example, the class theme has arisen from science then much of the writing and reading done in the language period will be about science.

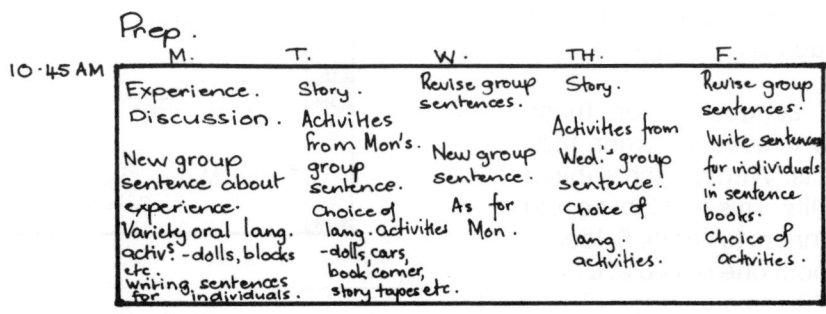

10.45 AM **Gr 2/3.**

> Teacher reads story, class expce. book or wall story.
> While teacher hears 6-8 children read individually, other chn. are involved with free reading, writing about expces, hand-writing (arising from needs), writing about photographs, word study activities, listening to story tapes, telling news or story onto tape, making a puppet play.
> All these activities would relate either to personal interests or the current class theme.

10.45 AM **Upper Grades.**

> Teacher or child reads story.
> Teacher takes shared book discussion with 6-8 children, or discusses individual books read with 6-8 children, while other chn. are involved in free reading, free writing, typing or re-writing stories, book making, handwriting for those needing practice, work on spelling errors, listening to tapes, conducting interviews, 3-4 chn cooking to a recipe, 3-4 chn. following directions to make a model. These activities would be related to class theme or indiv. interest.

SUMMARY

The language experience approach is an all encompassing method of language development. Not only do the child's listening, speaking, reading and writing develop out of his experiences, but this method enables the teacher to give instruction in phonics, handwriting and punctuation as the child shows a need, all in the context of the child's personal experiences. Teachers, like children, are individuals and work in different ways. Some will adopt an individualised teaching programme, while others will feel more comfortable with some group teaching and a quite consistent daily routine.

About the use of published materials

Children who learn to read by the language experience approach actually read published materials later than those who are taught the sight vocabulary of a particular reading scheme. This does not mean that they read at a later age, for they first read non published materials, that is their own utterances written for them by their teachers. Nor does it mean that in a language experience approach, children do not have access to published books. The opposite is true. The children are surrounded by and immersed in many high quality books. From their first days at school, children self-select and borrow the books which interest them. They may just look at and touch the pictures or verbalize a story from those pictures. Now, to get back to the non-published materials which the children will read. These include the teacher's transcription of children's own attempts at writing, the teacher's scribing of wall stories, experience books and room signs. From these activities each child gradually develops a sight vocabulary. He comes to know that the full context of the writing, he can name some of the words. But of course, a personal sight vocabulary cannot be an exact replica of the vocabulary of any one published reader. That is why I say that in a language experience approach, the reading of a published book by the child occurs later than where a child reads a book as a response to being taught all the sight words in the first weeks at school.

Teachers who are developing children's literacy from their experiences sometimes become anxious that their children are not reading and cannot read some of the simpler published books, when children from neighbouring schools can. Teachers need to be assured that the reading of non-published materials is in fact, reading. Reading does not always involve a published text—we read a letter from a friend, or re-read our lecture notes. It is most important that children keep reading personal reading materials until they can cope easily with simple published materials. Teachers need to keep expanding children's sight vocabularies through group sentences, wall stories, and transcribing individual utterances. Children need ready access to their own word cards, so that at any time they can get them out, make sentences with them, compare them with friend's words, and so on. As children's sight vocabularies expand they will realise that they can read some of the many published books in the classroom.

Child's Personal Story Book

Note how the cardboard back cover can be folded inward and stapled securely to form a pocket to store the child's sight vocabulary which has come from the child's utterances.

Parent Communication

Parents become anxious when their child is not reading a book like some other child who attends another school. It is both a valuable reading activity and a good public-relations exercise to send home duplicated reading books which consist of sentences arising from class experiences. For example, half a dozen of

the group sentences could be duplicated and stapled together into book form for the child to illustrate and then take home (see page 53).

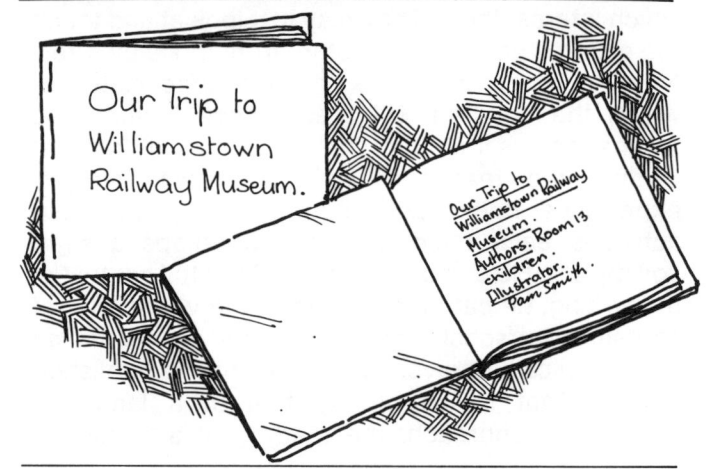

A wall story could be duplicated in book form, leaving room for each child to be his own illustrator. After a Grade 2 class visited a railway museum, many children contributed to a chalkboard story. The teacher duplicated the story in books and each child was able to take his copy home to read to his parents.

Teachers need to reassure parents that learning to read does not necessarily mean learning to read a particular reader. Parents who visit the classroom can see the wall charts, experience books, interest books and the children's personal experience books, all of which the children can read.

Interest Based Reading

Nevertheless, children who are learning to read by a language experience approach should not be divorced from published books. Attractive picture story books should be available in the classrooms. Children should be allowed to take home either library books or books from an interest-based scheme. An interest-based reading scheme is an organisation of reading materials into interest categories. The books may be fiction or non-fiction. Many of the books which are frequently called supplementary readers fit well into such a scheme. So do some magazines. The books are sorted according to content and difficulty. This makes it easier to relate what the child reads to the class experiences and interests. For example, if a group of children are studying cars, the teacher can have all the 'CAR' boxes from the interest-based scheme in her classroom. Thus an interest-based reading scheme combines well with an experienced-based approach.

Note that an interest-based reading scheme is not a method for teaching reading, but rather a way of organising reading materials. It is appropriate for use throughout the whole primary school. The teacher does not select the child's book, rather the child takes a book which he wants to read. Children choose books which interest them or which contain information they want. The books are sorted into three or four broad levels of difficulty so that the children can find something they can read. However no child is placed on a particular level, and children always select their own books.

When children take home books which they cannot read, it is wise to tell parents why: to help familiarise children with books and to have books seen as desirable and enjoyable. Parents sometimes believe that their children are failures because they take home books which they cannot read. These parents sometimes start exerting pressure on their children to learn to read, often producing anxiety and negative attitudes to reading.

Teachers may need to tell parents that pupils are encouraged to take home books of their choice primarily to get them interested in books and reading. Occasionally a parent needs to be told the value of sitting down with a child and reading the book to him, looking at the pictures and discussing the story.

It is worth reminding teachers and school administrators that if children are to develop a love of books, the books in the school must be attractive and appealing. Tatty, dirty books should be discarded regularly. Children who lose school books or return library books late should not be treated too harshly. I know a six-year-old boy who was banned in Term 1 from borrowing from his school library for the rest of the year. His crime was that he returned a beloved library book a week late. His pre-school sister had also delighted in this particular book so their mother had held onto it for a few extra readings. That little boy had so delighted in borrowing from the library and how heartbroken he was at the teacher's punishment.

The Aim of Teaching Reading

We should always remember that our aim in teaching reading is long term, in fact for the term of one's life. We should be cultivating a love of reading that will continue throughout the children's lifetimes and fill thousands of hours with pleasure. Short-term aims such as getting each child through a reading scheme, or making a child struggle unhappily through a book which he isn't enjoying may not contribute toward the achievement of a lifetime love of reading. Having each child complete every book that he begins can make reading a drag. If a book is uninteresting or badly written do you, as an adult, always finish it? Part of being able to discriminate in literature involves discussion of those books which we enjoy and those which we do not. The youngest child can give a reason why he doesn't like a book.

When children are allowed to choose the books they want to read (instead of taking the next book in a sequential reading scheme) they sometimes take books which are too difficult for them. Perhaps with those books they will just look at the pictures. In any case, they have the freedom to return any book which, for some reason or another, they do not want to finish. With practice, children become more particular in choosing their books.

The Importance of the Teacher Reading Aloud

As well as published books which the children can read for themselves the teacher reads aloud from a wide variety of picture story books, which are too difficult for the children to read for themselves. The teacher carefully selects books about different topics, by different authors, in differing language styles. By doing this the teacher is exciting children about books as well as showing them varied language models. Sometimes she makes a tape of a favourite book and leaves it in a cassette player, together with the book, so that interested children can read along with the tape.

SUMMARY

Children learn to read by a language experience approach. Their initial reading materials are their utterances written for them by their teachers. Together with these non-published books, children have access to good published books which may be part of an interest-based reading organisation, as well as to library books. At no time are children made to choose books at their level. If the aim in teaching reading is to have children love books so that they want to read for pleasure or to find information, then they must be able to select the book they want at that time. A girl who wants information about frogs may choose a very simple book if it contains the information she requires. That book may be way below her supposed reading level. We as adults chose a variety of materials to read. Sometimes we relax with a magazine; sometimes we struggle with a theoretical text. We don't always read at our highest level of ability. So with children, if they are to see reading as an enjoyable activity, let them gain confidence and pleasure through reading simple books or by re-reading a book they have previously enjoyed or let them grapple with difficult books, if they want to. As well, the teacher reads aloud frequently from good quality published books.

About the place of phonics

Which sound do you teach first?
Don't you teach phonics in a language experience approach?

I am frequently asked these questions and because I am unable to say which sound the children will learn first, or which letters the children will know by the end of their first year at school, the approach is seen to be phonicless! Phonics is an integral part of the language experience approach.

All too often teachers go about the teaching of literacy all back to front, perhaps they fail to see that reading involves meaning. These teachers proceed from the study of single sound/letter correspondences to the study of whole words and then to the study of phrases or sentences. If we remember that reading involves getting meaning from print, we begin with the child talking about his experiences and proceed to written language using the child's unit of meaning, that is the child's description of the experience, whether it is a couple of words, a sentence or a paragraph.

Only when a child indicates in some way that he is aware of smaller elements within the whole, that is individual words within the utterance, do teachers draw his attention to particular words. For example, the children may be asked to cover the outline of a word with cut paper, or to trace over the outline of a word or to find a word on a flash card in another place.

Similarly the teacher watches for signs that the child is beginning to notice elements within words, that is letters and sounds. The teacher then builds on what the child knows. An early sign that the child is noticing letters within words is when he points to a letter and says

That shape is in my name.

or

I see two shapes the same.

When the child makes a remark like that, the teacher could write that letter by itself and ask the child to find it written somewhere else in the room.

We See Letters. We Hear Sounds

It is very important to establish the difference between letters and sounds. One **sees** a letter; one hears a sound. One writes a letter which represents a particular sound. While it is true to say there are twenty-six letters in the English alphabet, it is not true to say there are only twenty-six sounds. It is generally agreed that there are about forty-four sounds. The precise number of sounds used by any English speaking person is dependent on dialect.

Letters Represent Sounds in the Context of Words

It is also important to note that a letter represents a sound only in the context of a word, and some words must be in the wider context of a sentence before the reader knows which sound a particular letter is representing. Such words are 'wind' and 'desert'. According to the context, letter 'i' in 'wind' represents different sounds, for example

The wind blows the leaves from the trees.
I wind the clock.

To instruct children that particular letters always represent particular sounds is poor teaching. For example, it is not accurate to have children call letter 'a' when written on a card by itself, the sound 'a' as in the word 'at'.

In 'was', letter 'a' represents 'o' sound as in 'dog'.
In 'can', 'a' represents 'a' sound as in 'cat'.
In 'away', the first 'a' represents the indefinite vowel or 'schwa' sound as in 'the'.

Remember that letters represent particular sounds only in the context of particular words. In the teaching of phonics we should be truthful right from the start. Many letters represent more than one sound. Many sounds are represented by more than one letter.

The approach, as described here, is that a study of sound letter correspondences grows out of the child's developing knowledge about written language and not vice versa. To study sounds and letters in the context of words which have come from personal utterances ensures understanding and purpose in the phonic programme.

Words are Made up of Sounds

The phonics programme begins when the teacher sounds the words as she writes the child's description of his experience. As the teacher is writing in front of the child, she sounds each word at the speed that she writes. The purpose of this practice is to have children know that words are made up of sounds; that sounds joined together can make words. Where children hear teachers sound words as they write them, they soon join in. When teachers hear children joining in, they encourage the practice with questions like the following,

The next word in your sentence is 'mother', what sound is at the start of 'mother'?
What is the next word in your sentence? — 'log'.
What is the first sound in 'log'?
What is the last sound in 'log'?
What is the middle sound in 'log'?
How many sounds are there in 'log'?
How many sounds are there in 'mother'?

Discovering a Letter

I said before that the teacher proceeds according to what the child notices or discovers. Let us now look at classroom practice when a child first discovers a letter. Arising from a class sentence 'We have new sand in the sand tray', one child might say

> I see two shapes the same.

The teacher could proceed as follows:

> Sally, come and point to the shape that you mean.

The child points to the letter 's'. The teacher would write the letter 's' by itself on the chalkboard. She would introduce the term 'letter'.

> Sally you call this a shape. The proper name for it is 'letter'.

The teacher would also introduce the name of the particular letter. The teacher would ask:

> Who has letter 's' in the name?

The children would then look for letters in room signs and labels.

The teacher could ask all the children in the group to go and find the letter in other labels and signs about the classroom.

The teacher would write the words containing letter 's' on the chalkboard.

Sally	Sue	flowers
sand	Saturday	
duster		

The teacher would then attempt to have the children relate letter 's' to the sound it is representing in those words.

The teacher would read each of those words in the list and then say:

> What sound do you hear the same in each of those words?

If the children are able to isolate the sound which is common to the words ('s'), she would then ask

> Who could underline the letter which is making the 's' sound in those words?

A child underlines letter 's' in each word.

Where the children are able to relate the letter to the sound they could participate in the following activities.

- Make a class list of words where letter 's' represents the 's' sound.

THE PLACE OF PHONICS

- In the children's personal sound/letter books the children could write letter 's' and either copy words from the 's' chart or draw objects whose names contain the 's' sound. The teacher would later label the drawings.

This would be an appropriate time to take a handwriting lesson regarding the correct formation of letter 's'.

If the children have difficulty relating a sound to the letter they discover, do not force the issue at this point. Introduce the term 'letter', and the particular letter name. Alert the children to look for the letter in other situations, for example street signs, grocery packets, room signs, etc.

Continue sounding words in front of the children as you write for them and occasionally play a sound game.

1. I Spy.
2. Sound Box. A sound box contains interesting little toys. A child selects a toy, says its name and tries to isolate the initial sound, for example 'Car starts with "c".'
3. Stand up when you hear a word beginning with 's'. Teacher says 'Cat, rabbit, seal, dog . . .' Sit down when you hear a word beginning with 'm'. Teacher says 'Lion, tiger, bear, monkey, . . .'

Discovering a Sound

Remember proceed according to what the child shows he understands at that time. If the child discovers a sound within a word but can't relate the sound to the corresponding letter, he does follow-up activities related to the sound. For example, he may draw objects in which he hears that sound.

When the phonic programme develops from the reading programme, children usually come to know combinations of letters and the sounds they represent, such as 'sh' in 'ship', 'ay' in 'play' and 'ck' in 'duck', before such a combination as 'x' in 'box'. The reason is that the children hear and see these former combinations more often.

When a phonic programme develops out of a child's reading programme, the child can see purpose in the study of sounds and letters. As children come to learn the various representations of sounds and are able to sound out words, they can begin writing for themselves. This is not to say that the child doesn't write at all before this. There are very definite stages that a child goes through in coming to write for himself. Several of the early stages are written in the child's personal code and cannot be read by anyone else (see pages 14-17). However, once children can sound out words slowly and have some knowledge of sound-symbol correspondence, they can write so that a person who is literate in English can read it back.

> The is uBaooT aool ~~skoot~~ skhool
> This wolkmen have to fiks
> ~~aoot aoot aool aoola aw~~ awl skhool

Note this seven-year-old's attempts to represent the 'ou' sound of 'about' and 'our'.

To have children work through every word on a three letter word list of the type below is to waste their time.

bog cog dog fog hog jog log tog
bid did kid lid mid rid

Once children have sound-symbol correspondence and can sound out words slowly, they can produce any of the words above in writing if they need them. This does not deny the value of sometimes looking at groups of words with common elements when the child has used one of the words in his writing. If the child writes

I saw the pig at the farm.

It might be appropriate to list with him 'pig', 'dig', 'big'.

> Do you know any other words which sound like this?
> What is the same about these words?
> What is different about these words?

Here the child's attention is being drawn to common elements within words but the words being studied are meaningful to him for they have come from his experience.

Phonics Arising from Errors Made in Writing
Initially the sound-symbol correspondences the child is studying will originate from his reading, but as he begins to write for himself, more and more phonic elements will come from his writing needs.
An eight-year-old wrote

> Yesday we went to the puk.

Several other children also wrote 'puk' for 'park' after the grade had been for a walk to the local park. The teacher then did some group teaching with these children. She asked them to identify the sounds in 'park' and then showed them the written representation of the word. Particular attention was drawn to the two letters representing the 'ar' sound. The teacher next listed other words where the letters 'ar' represented 'ar' sound.

arm car cart far farm star

Here the children's study of phonics was proceeding according to their needs as shown in their writing.

A class of Grade 2 children went to the film *Charlie and the Chocolate Factory*, after which they talked, wrote and drew about their experiences. From the children's writing it was evident that this was an appropriate occasion to study the 'ch' sound as in 'Charlie'. The children then compiled a long list of other 'ch' words.

Different Letters Can Represent One Sound

As children experience more writing and reading they will become familiar with several letter combinations which may represent one sound. A chart like the following may be compiled and extended later.

As well they will come to know that one letter may represent more than one sound as letter 'o' does in 'log', 'woman', 'women', 'only'.

READING AND THE PRACTICE OF SOUNDING OUT WORDS

There are three sources of information which the fluent reader draws upon in his endeavours to get meaning from print. They are syntactic, semantic and grapho-phonic.

The man . . . the dog.

In this sentence you will insert a verb in the space because your knowledge of grammar tells you that a verb is needed in the sentence. You have here drawn upon syntactic information.

The ship dropped . . .

In this example you will most probably insert the word 'anchor' in the space. Here you have drawn upon your knowledge about ships, and there aren't too many other things that a ship is likely to drop. In this example you have drawn upon semantic information. The fluent reader draws more frequently upon the syntactic and semantic cues than upon the graph-phonic or print cue. When hearing a child read do not encourage him to stop and sound out each word that he does not know. Sounding out slows down the reading process and makes meaning unattainable, because the child forgets what he read before. It is better to let the child draw upon his other two sources of information. Encourage him to either leave out or guess the unknown word and read to the end of the sentence. The child then asks himself, 'Did that make sense?' or 'What word would make sense in that space?' If the child is not successful in giving meaning to the passage, he reads the sentence again or reads back further for a clue to the unknown word. Here he is drawing upon context in his endeavours to get meaning from the text.

After the child has finished the passage the teacher might sometimes refer to one or two of the words he found difficult, and discuss their phonic elements. That is, the teacher might revise or introduce new phonic knowledge that is related to the child's immediate needs.

PERSONAL DICTIONARIES

When children begin writing for themselves and have some knowledge of the alphabet, the teacher can introduce personal dictionaries. These are exercise books with the alphabet entered one letter per page.

When a child needs a word in his writing but is rather unsure of the spelling, he first has a try at the word for himself, either on a scrap piece of paper or in the actual writing. Only when he has tried to write it for himself should he then check the spelling with the teacher. If the teacher tells children words for their personal dictionaries before the children have tried the words for themselves, the children will not practise their phonic knowledge. As well, the teacher misses the chance to see what the child does or does not know about sound-symbol correspondences. To relate the teaching of phonics or spelling to children's needs, it is necessary for children to try out words for themselves and to make errors. Only then can the teacher see which sound-letter correspondences or spelling rules are relevant to those children at that time.

For example where a child spells 'body' as 'bodee', from the child's writing, the teacher can see what the child does know, that is that the letters 'ee' represent the 'ee' sound as in 'tree'. The child has yet to learn that in some contexts letter 'y' represents the same 'ee' sound.

However, the child who spells 'body' as 'boddy' has a different spelling need.

SUMMARY

The study of phonics is an integral part of the language experience programme. In the beginning literacy programme teachers sound words as they write them in context, thus providing the information that words are made up of sounds. The study of sound-letter relationships begins when the children comment upon particular sounds or letters in the reading programme. There is no pre-determined order for the introduction of sounds or letters. When children begin writing for themselves, the study of sound-letter relationships develops from the errors they make in their writing.

I would like too be an elephant so I can throw water over my back too keep it cool then I would be cool on my back I woul lik too # if I was a elephant I would drink watter and eat food too I would have a long nose I can give chidren a ride on my back If I wasnt an elephant I would get boring and hot too my faces would get very swetay too. Rachele.

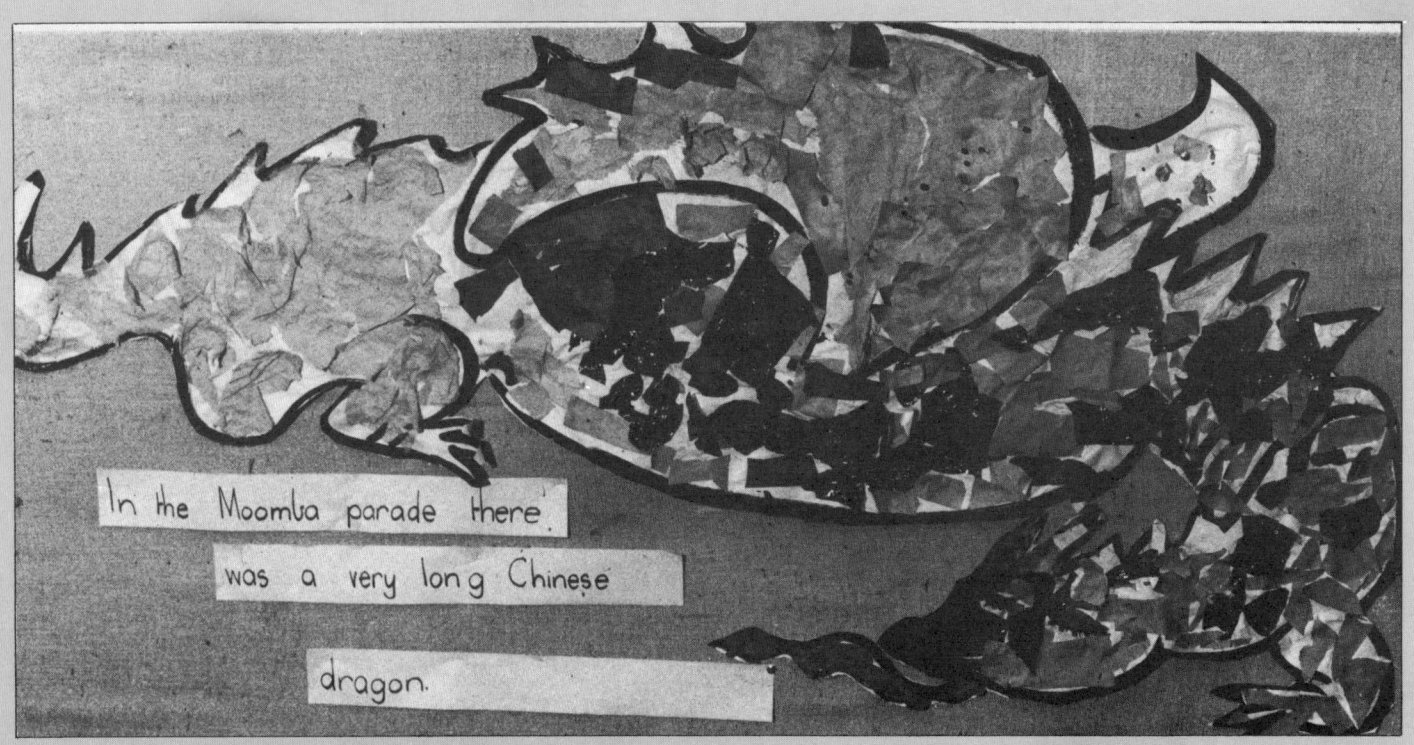

A suggested literacy course outline

The following developments in literacy are not exclusive from one another nor are they tightly sequential.

WRITING is putting down thoughts in visual symbols, and the way the symbols are made (usually called Handwriting).

READING, in brief, is getting meaning from print.

Teaching Points	Development in Writing	Development in Reading	Teaching Points
(a) The children must see much written language about their classroom, so they come to know what it looks like. For example > Please shut the door. > The scissors go here. (b) Children must learn that what they say may be written and what is written can be read back. The teacher might say, 'That was an interesting story you told me, may I write it for you?' (c) As the teacher writes in front of the children, she introduces technical terms such as 'write', 'read', 'words', 'sentences'.	**That children will know what writing is.** Why should a child want to learn to write if he does not know what writing is?	**That children will know what reading is.** Why should a child want to learn to read if he does not know what reading is?	(a) For those children who do not know what reading is, because no-one has read to them at home, or perhaps because their parents cannot read, the teacher must inform them what reading is by reading to them. She must instruct them which part of the book tells her what to say—the print not the pictures. (b) There must be an adequate supply of attractive books for the children to handle. (c) The teacher could sometimes sit in the book corner reading and discussing books with individual children. She uses words such as, 'book', 'read', 'page', 'print'.

77

Teaching Points	Development in Writing	Development in Reading	Teaching Points
The teacher has to convey to the children there is purpose and value in being able to write. Here are some ideas. 1 One can leave a message for someone. > Do not touch. Wet paint. 2 One can write a letter to a friend via a room or school postal service. 3 One can write a notice to explain a display. > John, Frank and Jo made a swimming pool. See how they used ice-cream sticks for steps. 4 One can write a story-book for others to read. 5 One can leave a sign on a construction to protect it. > Do not break this building.	**That children will see value for them in learning to write.**	**That children will see value for them in learning to read.**	The teacher has to convey to the children the value and purpose in being able to read. 1 She reads aloud frequently from good quality books so children see that reading is enjoyable. 2 Signs placed by activity areas tell something of value. > You may add water to the sand today. or > Come to me and I'll give you cars for the sand-tray. > Miss Browning

WRITE ME A SIGN

Teaching Points	Development in Writing	Development in Reading	Teaching Points
As the teacher writes the child's utterance she comments about the starting place. She asks the child to point to the side of the page where she will begin, and as well to point in the direction the writing will go.	**The children will come to know the directional nature of our written language; that written English moves from left to right across the page and progressively down the page.**		When the teacher reads to the children, she shows them where she begins reading, and the direction she will follow.
The teacher uses these words as she writes for the children. She might ask the child to put his hand over a word, or to count the number of words in the sentence.	**That children will come to be familiar with the technical vocabulary of literacy.** 'word', 'letter', 'sentence', 'write', 'print', 'full-stop', 'book', 'page', 'read', 'sound'.		When reading to children, the teacher makes use of some of these words.

Teaching Points	Development in Writing	Development in Reading	Teaching Points

(a) The child's first attempts at writing might be
 	
1 Scribble
2 Personal or non-conventional letters
 	
`PT 9ε9α α9F ⊥ℓ`
 	
3 Strings of conventional letters
 	
`DIterher. DIEIm`
 	
4 Groups of letters with spaces between
 	
`WP  PS(( 7HK  Lo19`
`AGTn  DPY  m  gr.`
`Bq.tV  ehc       >`
 	
5 Writing which reveals developing knowledge of sound/symbol correspondences
 	
> We wet to da puk.
> (We went to the park.)
 	
(See **(b)** opposite.)
	That children will attempt to write for themselves before being able to write.	That children will attempt to read for themselves before being able to read.	**(a)** The child's first attempts at reading may be
			
			1 'Reading back' his early attempt at writing.
			2 'Reading' what the teacher has written.
			3 'Reading' from a book which may be invention or memorisation.
			
			(b) All these early attempts at reading are encouraged and the teacher provides feedback appropriate to the child's understanding. For example if the child 'reads' from the picture, the teacher shows the child how she reads the print.
			
			(b) All of these early attempts at writing are encouraged and the teacher provides feedback appropriate to the child's level of understanding.
			
			(c) Parallel with this personal development in writing, the child copies over and traces beneath the adult writing model
			
			> We went to the zoo.
			> we went to the zoo.

80 *WRITE ME A SIGN*

Teaching Points	Development in Writing	Development in Reading	Teaching Points
(a) As children build up personal sight vocabularies, together with knowledge about sound/symbol correspondences, their writing will reflect their increasing word knowledge. (b) Children can be encouraged to check the spelling of words used in their writing, against their personal word cards. (See (b) opposite.) (c) When writing, children should always have a try at words for themselves, before seeking assistance from the teacher.	**That children will come to identify individual words in reading and attempt to write them when writing.**		(a) Once the child has a concept of a word, the teacher asks him to identify particular words. For example if the child's sentence is > My mum is sick. the teacher asks the child to point to 'sick'. (b) When a child can identify a particular word in a sentence, the teacher writes the word on a card for him. The child is now developing a sight vocabulary > sick Children's sight words may be stored in a shoe tidy (see page 54). (c) Children will come to draw on several cues for the identification of words when reading 1 Syntactic. 2 Semantic. 3 Grapho-phonic. As well, children may look at the picture for information about the text. (See (d) opposite.)
(From (d) opposite.) (d) When reading, children should be encouraged to draw upon all these sources of information and read to make sense, or read to make meaning from the text. Teachers should not tell a child each word he does not know, nor should they make the child stop and sound out the word. Rather the child should guess at a word which will make sense in the space. That is the child is required to draw upon syntactic and semantic information and read to make sense.			

Teaching Points	Development in Writing	Development in Reading	Teaching Points
(a) When writing in front of the children the teacher says the word, then sounds it as she writes it. This practice conveys the message that words are made up of sounds. **(b)** Early in their first year of school, some children will join in the sounding of words, as the teacher writes for them. This is encouraged. **(c)** By constantly hearing words being sounded, children will come to isolate some sounds. (See **(d)** opposite.)	**That children will come to know words are made up of sounds.**		**(d)** This identification of sounds is fostered by activities such as The next word is 'dog'. What do you hear at the start of 'dog'? What do you hear at the end of 'dog'?
(a) Letters only represent sounds in the context of words, and therefore the study of phonics arises out of words with which the children are familiar. **(b)** For children who can blend sounds together to make words, the job of writing down words becomes much easier. Of course the child's knowledge of sound/letter correspondences together with pronounciation will determine the accuracy of the child's spelling: elephant or elefunt. (See **(c)** opposite.)	**That children will be able to blend the sounds of the English language.** For the purpose of sounding out words when reading and putting down words when writing, children will come to join sounds together, that is blend.		**(c)** Where a child requests help in the spelling of a word, the teacher may say Say 'park' slowly. What was the first sound? What was the second sound? What was the last sound? How many sounds in 'park'? (Britton, 1970.)

Teaching Points	Development in Writing	Development in Reading	Teaching Points

(a) We hear sounds. We cannot write them. We write letters which represent sounds.
 	
(b) For a child, the study of sound/symbol correspondences begins when he says,
 	
   I see two shapes the same in that sentence.
 	
or
 	
   That shape is in my name.
 	
or
 	
   I hear 's' in 'school' and 'sand'.
 	
These comments are usually made as the teacher is writing a sentence for a group or individual.
   The shape (letter) or sound noticed by the child is talked about and studied in greater depth for example a sound chart may be started.
 	
(c) As some digraphs occur more frequently in word usage than some single letters, children learn these before less frequently used single sound/letter combinations, for example most children are familiar with 'sh' and 'ay' before 'x'.
(See opposite.)
	That children will come to know the sound symbol correspondences of the English language.		**(d)** When children study digraphs, or two letters together representing one sound (sh), it is important that they know the names of the letters, so they may converse accurately about them. Many children will know the letter names before they will be using digraphs.
			
			(e) A child's phonic programme arises from words he meets in reading and from errors he makes in writing. For example where the child writes 'trane', he could be introduced to 'ai' as in 'train', 'mail', 'rain'.
			
			(f) Class lists of word groups should be displayed
			
			   train stain
			   rain mail
			   pain rail
			
			(g) When children know various representations of the one sound, charts of this type may be compiled
			
			--- 	
			ay ai a-e
			
			--- 	
			hay train came
			day rain gate
			play pain hate
			--- 	

Teaching Points	Development in Writing	Development in Reading	Teaching Points
(a) When the teacher first writes for the children she comments on the use of the capital letter and full-stop. When children begin writing they are then familiar with these writers' conventions. **(b)** When it is relevant for particular children the teacher introduces 'comma', 'direct speech', 'question mark'. **(c)** Capital letters are used for people and place names, also for days of the week.	That children will come to know in order to facilitate communication via written language certain printers' conventions are observed.		**(a)** When listening to children read from books, the teacher occasionally refers to the use of 'capital letters', 'full stop', 'question mark', etc. She comments about their function.
(a) It is a courtesy when writing for others, that the writing is easily read. **(b)** Children do need instruction in letter formation and in setting out of work. **(c)** Practice in letter formation may begin when children isolate particular letters as part of their phonic programme. **(d)** Once children are writing for themselves, the teacher relates teaching of handwriting to needs revealed in the children's writing.	That children will come to take care with the presentation of their writing. The child will write legibly so that the reader is not retarded in his efforts to read for meaning by poor letter formation or sloppy presentation.	That when children are required to read aloud to others they will realise the importance in taking care with the presentation of their oral reading.	**(a)** Whenever the teacher reads aloud she takes care with tone of voice, speed of reading, characterisation and facial expressions. **(b)** Children should be encouraged to read aloud to the grade. 1 A favourite book. 2 An exciting paragraph. 3 An interesting article from a newspaper. 4 A story written by the child.

Teaching Points	Development in Writing	Development in Reading	Teaching Points
(a) A child will proof-read his own writing. When writing, the child puts a dot or line under any word about which he is uncertain. He later checks for meaning or spelling, in a dictionary. (b) Use of published dictionaries should be encouraged. (c) Class magazines, class books, school newspapers, books for younger children to read, can provide motivation for accuracy. (d) Further writers' conventions are introduced 1 Capital letters for countries, states, street names, months. 2 Exclamation mark, contractions. 3 Paragraphing. 4 Indexing. 5 Letter-writing.	That the child will write with greater accuracy.	That the child will become more efficient at gaining meaning from print.	(a) The teacher ensures the child meets a wide variety of reading materials, paper back novels, award winning books, magazines, newspapers. (b) Discussion of what is read occurs frequently. Children are challenged to find criteria for what is good reading matter. (c) The child is expected to respond on three levels of comprehension, literal, interpretive and critical. (d) Children will need practice at retrieving material from phone books, street directories, dictionaries, encyclopaedias, etc. (e) Children need to be able to find materials in a library, fiction, non-fiction, etc. How to use a catalogue. (f) Use of non-published reading materials should be continued right through the primary school. All children love reading about themselves. 　　As well older, slower readers will read more easily their oral language which has been written for them, than published books.

Teaching Points	Development in Writing	Development in Reading	Teaching Points
(a) The teacher varies the audience for whom the child is asked to write. Sometimes the child writes 1 For himself. 2 For others, either in the familiar or unfamiliar style. (b) The teacher varies the purpose of the writing 1 Report writing. 2 Imaginative writing. 3 Letter-writing, complaining, appealing, apologising, etc. 4 An article for a magazine. 5 Writing showing visual, sound, and symbolic qualities of language. 6 Writing to summarise. 7 Book reviewing.	**That the child will be able to write and read for different purposes.**		The teacher varies the purpose for which the children are asked to read. 1 Reading for detail, for example reading a recipe. 2 Reading for underlying meaning, for example a novel. 3 Reading to skim; for example does this book have the information I require.
The teacher observes Do the children enjoy writing? Do they vary the purpose of their writing? Do they write voluntarily? Do they write outside school hours?	**That the child will leave primary school with favourable attitudes to writing and reading.** Children should leave primary school seeing writing and reading as highly desirable, enjoyable, activities.		The teacher observes Do the children enjoy reading? Do they read for different purposes? Do they read voluntarily? Do they borrow books from the school library? Do they read at home? Do they belong to the community library?

a grey egg with blue and red stripes.

a purple
 with
 ange
 lines.

a red egg with green ribbon

Appendix I
A case study: Language for thinking

A CASE STUDY: LANGUAGE FOR THINKING

I present now, in sequence, the writings of a girl who was in her second year at school. She was an intelligent Australian pupil of literate parents. Her first year of schooling was spent at a large country school. She enrolled at the Helen Street School at the start of her second year of schooling.

From her earliest days at Northcote, it was estimated that Mary was an intelligent pupil for she was reading and spoke fluently and confidently. However her written language did not match our expectations. Here are some samples of her early writings.

February 18

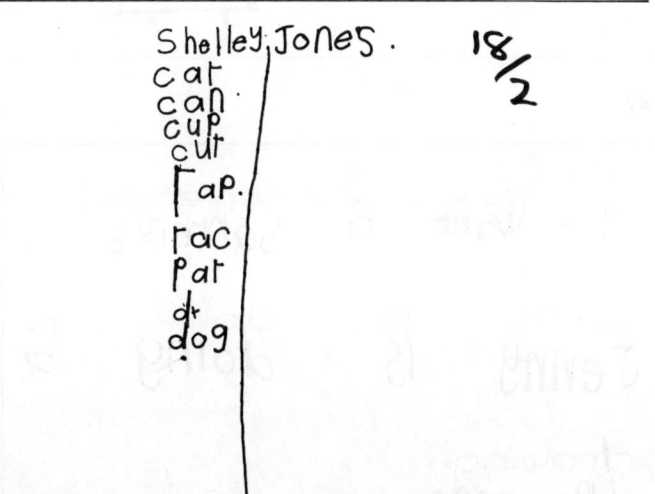

This writing was done during free time. No instruction was given to write words.

18 February

Dictated for the teacher to write.

27 February

Dictated for the teacher to write, after a trip to the beach.

1 March

Written by Mary.

3 March

May

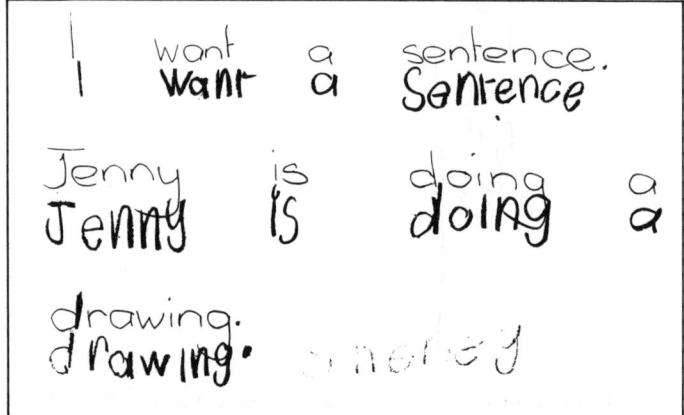

Dictated for the teacher to write.

May

We went up High Street
we went up High Street
and we saw Julie A. On
dnd We saw Julie A on

Easter night my daddy took
Easter night my daddy took

some meat for the cats
some meat for the cats
in the factory. Daddy
in the factory Daddy
has two cats in the factory
has two cats in the factory
Mummy works in the jewellery
Mummy works in the jewellery

factory and she makes
factory and she makes
blue bird necklaces and
blue bird necklaces and
she makes blue bird badges
She makes blue bird badges.

Dictated for the teacher to write.

June

my mum is doing
her work DaviD is
a good boy
Shelley is A good
girl Alex is a good
boy Tenny and Alex
kiss Lazo is a Naugty
boY DaViD is a good
boY rob is a good
boy too.

Written by Mary.

July

Tulle and Fat Alex kiss to geTher
David is doing his hud work
Tenny is a good girl
Mileva is a good girl
Tulle is a good Scrag

Written by Mary.

August

This greek grand mother kiss all of the children I can see all of the children in the picture But I can not see David and rob in the picture.

Written by Mary.

27 September

I went in a car and my nanna And Sheroll and I had a hide on a houes and 2 cats and 3 dog and 5 houes and I had a ride on a houes and They was big houes and Drarck went to ~~sc~~ School and Thats all

Written by Mary.

When Mary commenced at our school she was reading many of the well known early basal readers, and was most fluent and confident with spoken language. However when she was asked to write or asked to dictate for the teacher to write, her language became very stilted. Almost invariably her written sentences were of the 'This is . . .' type. During April and May she stopped trying to write for herself and asked the teacher to write at her direction. Notice how she begins in the May example.

'I want a sentence'. She is now confident in the knowledge that the teacher will write for her exactly what she wants written. The utterances will not be changed or 'improved' by the adult and the teacher does not mind writing for her. In this particular example Mary has got away from the 'This is . . .' pattern but there is no great depth to her writing.

We see in the next May example that Mary is beginning to use writing in a more meaningful fashion. She dictated this piece for the teacher to write and is writing about her mother and father.

Mary went through several months where she wrote for herself but wrote continually about people being good or bad. Adjustment to her new school had not been easy for her. It appears that she was re-establishing values for herself as to what was good and what was bad. To be active and inquisitive and to question and to write freely were good things in her new school situation. From the report that came from her former school, quietness, passivity and neatness were the qualities valued there.

In August and September she writes less and less about 'good' or 'bad' and uses writing to report on her experiences. Notice in her September writings that there are more words spelt incorrectly than in her earlier writings. Until September Mary was overly concerned with having everything spelled correctly. She constantly asked her teacher those words she needed in her writing and would not have a try at them for herself. For Mary writing had not been a medium where she could freely express her thoughts for she had been too concerned with aspects of the surface structure. Where children are encouraged and praised for their very early writings and encouraged to discuss the content, they very quickly come to realise that writing holds no fears for them and are able to use writing to write about their worlds.

Contrast Mary's writings with that of Margaret. She voluntarily did this writing and then gave it to her teacher to read. It is possible that Margaret has been requested not to tell at school what happened at home, but she is a concerned little girl and the domestic situation is too much for her shoulders alone. She was able to get this week's crisis off her chest by writing about it and putting that writing in the hands of someone she could trust. Lack of sophistication with the surface structure of our language has not prevented Margaret from using writing to freely express her thoughts.

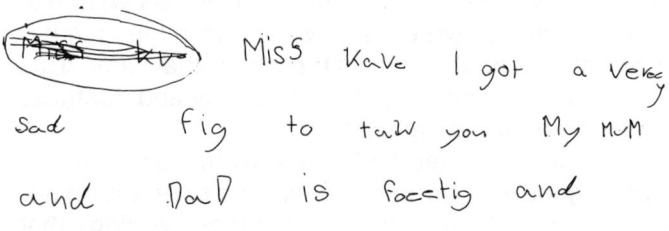

sdudot and My MuM D,Dnt Hav The Dinu reDec and wenan My Dad wonood The Dinu redce and Then My Atee um ovr. My Hosloos and She saw The Black orecy and wend. My Antee cumcem I was in the lanshroomym and I Dindo now She wos cumonre and vendcn The Peepool Hood The focet The END

Margaret is in her third year at school. In her first two years violent tantrums indicated to us that all was not well at home and when she was calm she would talk about her troubles. On this occasion she felt confident enough with her writing to pour it all out on paper and give it to her teacher. This time there was no tantrum and no discussion about the fight.

Appendix II
Checklist of dos and don'ts

CHECK LIST OF DOS AND DON'TS

Dos

1. Do arrange your classroom so that it is a stimulating environment for children. The classroom environment should make children want to talk. It should entice them to get involved. A classroom where the only equipment is a collection of desks is a very sterile environment for children.
2. Do read aloud every day to the children. This applies to upper grades as well as to infant children. Remember that there are two modes of input of language and one of these is by listening. Children's knowledge about language is expanded by hearing it. If you are going to read a serial story to older children do make it a daily event rather than a weekly one.
3. Do find something to praise about every child in your class. Good self images are very important in the learning process.
4. Do examine the number and types of direct experiences which you include in your learning programme. Is there a good balance of in and out of school experiences? Do plan for social experiences. Remember to include aesthetic experiences, such as visits to galleries, the cinema and theatre.
5. Do teach to children's needs. Observe your children so you know what they are capable of doing and when they are ready to be extended in their learning.
6. When writing a child's utterance for him, do write it exactly as he says it. If the child is to make a match between the written and spoken forms of his utterance, then it must be written as it is spoken.
7. Do set aside time each week to hear read or read with those children who are not confident readers. I suggest that children who are learning should be heard read a minimum of twice a week.
8. Do encourage the child who is reading to read for meaning. You might say to him,

   > Tell me the story in your own words.
   > Did you like the ending to that story? Could you make up a better ending?
   > Did that make sense?

9. Do let the children select the book which they want to read and take home. Initially this means the children may choose books which are too difficult for them to read, but being free to look at a range of books will help the child come to know his own capabilities in reading.

10 Do make lots of class experience books. Of course older children will write for themselves. Topics might include,
Children in our class (use photos).
Teachers at our school (use photos).
Things we like doing.
Things we don't like doing.
Excursions.
Favourite footballers.

A photo book of the children in the class is an excellent experience book for the start of the school year. Not only can the children read about themselves but the teacher can use this book to get to know her pupils.

Don'ts
1 As the teacher in the room, don't be the person who does all or most of the talking.
2 Don't expect the children to talk or write with feeling and understanding about something which they have not experienced.
3 Don't put all the migrant children in one class and the English speaking pupils in another. Children learn language by hearing it spoken. Migrant pupils learn English from English speaking pupils as well as from English speaking teachers.
4 Don't make a child labour through a book which he either doesn't like or which is too difficult for him. Remember that you want him to like reading! If he is interested in a book but can't read it, you read it for him.
5 Don't record the readers which a child has read on the inside of his reader cover. This can cause unhealthy competition between parents about whose child has read most books. This in turn can lead to children borrowing easy or thin books just so they can get through them quickly and have additional ticks recorded on their reader cover.
6 Don't waste children's time with time filling activities. Many roneod sheet activities are of little or no intellectual value and merely serve to keep children quiet. Many 'Read and Draw' and 'Fill the Gap' chalkboard exercises are similarly just busy activities and do not serve to promote interest in, or development through, reading.
7 Don't waste children's time with a daily handwriting lesson. If particular letter formation is poor, do teach it. Take a lesson aimed at correcting that poor formation. If the children write neatly and form letters well it is to waste their time to continue to take that daily handwriting lesson.
8 Don't make writing a chore. Try to have a variety of media available for expressive activities. Don't spoil every excursion by making all children write about it afterwards.
9 Don't be more interested in how a child writes something than in what he writes.

References

Barnes, D. (1976), *From Communication to Curriculum*, Penguin, Harmondsworth.

Britton, J. (1970), *Language and Learning*, Penguin, Harmondsworth.

Buettner, C. (1962), *Bozo the Clown*, Golden Press, Sydney.

Goodman, K. (1973), Psycholinguistic universals in the reading process, *in* F. Smith (ed), *Psycholinguistics and Reading,* Holt, Rinehart and Winston, New York.

The 'Happy Trio' Reading Scheme, from We work and play, Wheaton, Exeter.

Learning English in Australia, from *Reader 18* David's morning at the station, AGPS, Canberra.

Marshall, S. (1963), *An Experiment in Education*. Cambridge University Press, Cambridge.

Postman, N. and Weingartener, C. (1972), *Teaching as a Subversive Activity*, Penguin, Harmondsworth.

Smith, F. (1971), *Understanding Reading*. Holt, Rinehart and Winston, New York.

Strickland, R. (1970), Building on what we know, in *The New Era*, August.

Index

Deep structure of language, 17,18,47

Experiences, 11,32-33,37-44
Expressive activities, 27-29

Handwriting, 52

Individual differences, 3,19,20
Individual story books, 53-54,61
Interest based reading, 62-64
Interrelationships of listening, speaking,
    reading and writing, 21

Language and learning, 12-14
Language experience
    definition, 11
    group approach, 48-53
    initial literacy, 48-55
    structure, 23
    whole school approach, 11
Letters and sounds, 67-71

Motivation for reading and writing, 2-8

Objectives, 77-86
Oral language, 27-34
    acquisition, 14
    adult feedback, 29-30,33
    components of programme, 29-33

Parent communication, 62,63
Personal dictionaries, 73
Phonics, 50,51,52,67-74
    and reading, 72-73
Published materials, 61-65

Questioning, 30-31

Reading
    aim, 63-64
    meaning, 47
    process, 21,22
    readiness, 22
    aloud, 64
Room arrangement, 32

Surface structure of language, 17,18,19,47,94

Timetabling, 55

Wall stories, 48-49,62
Writing
    development of, 14-17